THE TRUE INDIA

THE TRUE INDIA:

A PLEA FOR UNDERSTANDING

C. F. ANDREWS

GYAN

Published by

GYAN

Gyan Publishing House
5, Ansari Road
Daryaganj, New Delhi-110002
Phone: 011-47034999, 9811692060
E-mail: books@gyanbooks.com

Distribution Network
gyanbooks.com
India, USA, Canada, UK, Australia

ISBN: 978-93-6920-302-4 (PB)

First Published, 1939

2nd Impression 2025

Printed at: Gyan Press, Delhi.

THE TRUE INDIA
Author: C. F. ANDREWS

THE TRUE INDIA

THE TRUE INDIA

A Plea for Understanding

by

C. F. ANDREWS

To the Poet

RABINDRANATH TAGORE

with deep affection

PREFACE

For more than ten years, a succession of books has come from the Press both in America and Great Britain condemning the morals of India and pointedly attacking Hinduism as a debased religion.

These have caused great offence in India itself, and have led to very serious misunderstanding. The replies that were published in India had only a small circulation, and therefore the misunderstanding has remained. India's own case has very nearly gone by default.

For this reason I have often been urged, as a friend of India, to make known the truth as I have seen it, so that those who desired in all sincerity to know the facts might be able to do so. After long hesitation, it seemed to me at last that the time had come to undertake this, and therefore this book has been written.

In these days of world bitterness and confusion, it is more than ever necessary for peace-lovers to build up, wherever possible, bulwarks of sincere good-will to withstand the inrushing tide of hatred between nations. Sensational and unfair literature does immeasurable harm by stirring up hostility among masses of people who feel that their own country and their own religion have both been unjustly attacked. Naturally their desire has been to answer back. But mere retaliation can do no good, and what I have aimed at is to build up a constructive picture of Indian life which shall express the truth and at the same time expose some of the fallacies on which this sensational literature has been based.

In the final revision of this book I have had most valuable help from Indian and English friends to whom I have been able to show the manuscript for advice and correction. My friend, John Mathew, has won my gratitude for his excellent typing. Ill-health has compelled me to finish my task at a small hill station, where it has been impossible to verify references, but I hope that no inaccuracies have crept into my text. In certain chapters I have used the material of articles which I had already contributed to the public press.

In dedicating what I have written to the poet, Rabindranath Tagore, I am seeking to repay a very small portion of the debt which I owe to him for opening my eyes both to the deeper meaning of Indian culture and to the singular beauty of the lives of the simple villagers who bear such heavy burdens with a cheerfulness and nobility of spirit that often puts us all to shame. Tagore knows and loves Indian village life best of all, and his simple songs will live on the lips of many generations of the country folk long after other memorials have perished.

C. F. ANDREWS

KOTAGIRI

CONTENTS

INTRODUCTION

While I was travelling recently on a world tour undertaken in connexion with the Student Christian Movement, I was surprised and pained to discover what desolating harm had been done to the cause of international good-will by a certain type of literature which has given an entirely one-sided impression of Indian moral life to-day as being altogether decadent and corrupt. The Hindu religion itself has been the centre of the attack. Unfortunately, this wrong done to India has been increased in the West by paragraphs in certain missionary publications of a crude type, setting forward the darker side of Hinduism and Islam with very little appreciation of what is good in those religions.

This one-sided presentation, through the Press and on the platform, continuing year after year, has tended to throw the truth about India out of focus. The *real* India becomes obscured. A false perspective has been given.

While it is happily true that in the missionary sphere great improvement has taken place and the majority of missionaries seek to be fair and impartial, it is also true that there are still controversialists among them who seem unable to resist the opportunity, when they reach their home environments, of carrying on the old, bad method of decrying other religions in a way that Christ Himself would have been the very first to condemn. For His own words are as clear as possible, that He came not to destroy, but to fulfil.

Not long ago in London a film was to be produced professing to represent a cinema picture of Indian life. This film was regarded as entirely unobjectionable by its missionary producers. But when a copy of the scenario was shown to me, I was able to point out at once certain things that were obviously out of date, and therefore bound to give needless offence to good people who were Hindu by birth. Note was taken of this, and they were immediately omitted. Such an instance as this has been quoted merely to show what precautions are needed where naturally a keen sensitiveness exists. Indian sentiment surely ought to be respected by those whose one desire is to reveal to mankind the spirit of their Master, Jesus Christ.

When I came out to India as a missionary thirty-five years ago this mode of attack on other religions was fairly common. The effort was constantly made to show up the seamy side of things. In still earlier days the habit was even more pronounced. At one time, when I had to make research into early missionary literature for the purpose of writing a book on North India, I was profoundly shocked by the things I read in print. I remember also being given at Delhi, soon after my arrival, a whole series of pamphlets published by a missionary who had been employed at a station not far distant. These contained nothing but a number of bitter attacks upon what were considered to be the vulnerable points in the armour of Hinduism. Such a form of controversy led on to counter-attacks. Abuse was poured upon the Christian religion in turn. It was something like the modern armaments race, in which more and more destructive weapons are produced till at last open war ensues.

I wish that I could assert with full confidence that all this kind of controversy had been done away with for ever; for it is utterly unchristian. But now and then, especially in the home countries, these objectionable methods are still employed at meetings where there is no one to put forward the other side of the case. The distress and indignation which such practices cause can easily be imagined.

It needs to be added, in order to make clear the change that has taken place, that lately very notable work has been done, under direct missionary auspices, of exactly the opposite kind. Some of the finest gems of Hindu literature, such as the songs of Tukaram, have been edited and translated in such a way as to make them fully appreciated almost for the first time in the West. The works of Nicol Macnicol, Jack Winslow, and J. S. Hoyland are in this respect worthy of note, and also those of Verrier Elwin. Genuine love has been put into their translations, and the publication of these Hindu classics by those who came out to India as missionaries has done much in Europe and America to remove the false impression created by other kinds of literature.

But sadly enough the different Christian denominations, which send out men and women to India, are scattered and divided. There is no single standard of training and discipline which is universally observed. The National Christian Council of India has sought lately with some success to co-ordinate missionary effort, but much is still being done which cannot be brought under its control. The great Roman Catholic Church, with its high standard of sacrifice and devotion, remains almost entirely apart and aloof. Therefore a deplorable rivalry has taken place, with painfully disintegrating results. The Indian Church has suffered in consequence.

These attacks on Hindu morals have been regarded by Indians themselves as a subtle form of politics whose main ulterior object was to prove that Indians, who have such bad morals, are not ready for self-government. The evil thus begun and carried on through a large number of publications reached its climax in a new book by Miss Mayo, with pictures representing Hinduism at its worst, which the British Government in India very rightly refused to allow to enter the country. Its immediate proscription was a prudent measure taken at a critical juncture; for it would have been certain to have stirred up once more the old bitter recrimination just after it had died down.

It is not that Indians themselves desire either to conceal or condone the things that are wrong in their ancient social and religious organizations. Nothing could possibly exceed the frankness with which they have unreservedly exposed abuses, dragging them forward relentlessly into the light for scathing rebuke. Nor do they in the very least object to those who have already been proved to be their friends pointing out that which is harmful. Miss Rathbone's book, for instance, on child marriage, called *The Indian Minotaur*,[1] which gave accurate statistics concerning this evil, was welcomed by the All India Women's Conference. But they do object very strongly indeed to people coming from the outside as foreigners, and then after a short cold weather visit going back to the West to exaggerate in glaring colours these evils before the world with no sense of proportion and with no presentation of the other side of the picture. To do this is all the more unfair, as power and prestige are behind these Western writers, while they attack those who have no opportunity of making an effective reply.

To return to my own experience in different parts of the world concerning the wide spread of this abusive, anti-Hindu literature, it came to me, as I have said, with a great shock of surprise to find that this entirely distorted picture of Hinduism was still being widely regarded as authoritative in every country I visited. My surprise was extreme because I had wrongly supposed that such sensational material as this, which had been so hastily collected, would have been discredited long ago. But here was *Mother India* being sold all over the world in a cheap edition, even on railway bookstalls, and having an honoured place in the libraries of private persons. Furthermore, I found that it had been published in

[1] *Child Marriage: The Indian Minotaur* (George Allen & Unwin Ltd.)

different translations in foreign countries. Indeed, so large had been the circulation that even to-day, after all its numerous editions, it appears to be about to start on a new career of sale in the world market. For the volume has taken its place, among the list of "famous authors," in a series of books which are to be retailed at popular prices.

It may be well, therefore, to relate in further detail some of the personal experiences which I have had as to the harm done to India's reputation abroad by such sales. For this fact has to be driven home. More than anything else it has made me feel the need, in the cause of truth, of presenting the other side of the picture. For what is now being offered to the public is often a menace to good-will and friendship between East and West.

(1) In New Zealand I met the Indian Community at Auckland, Wellington, and Christchurch, and also the Indian students at Auckland and Dunedin. Among the thoughtful New Zealanders there were many who were deeply interested in India and anxious to do her people full justice. All of these were indignant at the misrepresentations which were still being published. For their own use, in their daily intercourse with other people, there was required some simple and constructive book that might state in a brief compass the real truth about Hindu morals and religion. For they explained to me what difficulty they had in counteracting these scurrilous attacks.

(2) In Fiji, which is near to New Zealand and

where there is a large Indian population, this propaganda had done great harm by stirring up racial prejudice at a time when nothing was more supremely needed than racial good-will and friendship.

(3) In Australia a similar experience awaited me. Indians who were resident in Sydney, Melbourne, Perth, and other places spoke of the harm that was being done by this adverse view of India which had recently been created. It has stirred up all the worst prejudices of "White Australia." When I lectured about India in the great cities references were made to the bad effect on the public mind of this kind of literature. Those who were on the side of India in her struggle for self-government asked me on many occasions to give them some reliable account of Indian morals which might undo the evil that had already been done by sensational literature.

(4) When I was in Berlin a German lady brought me an article written in one of the leading newspapers. It was full of cruelly misleading statements. She asked me to contradict it in the same paper, and I did so. Here it was a mere accident that I was present in Berlin at that particular moment. Otherwise the article would have been regarded by most people as authoritative.

(5) When I have been lecturing in Canada and the United States I have been cross-questioned after the lecture was over by those who had read attacks upon Indian morals which had their origin in this form of writing. So many books of the same type have appeared, since *Mother India* reached its

phenomenal circulation, that many erroneous views are now regarded by a vast multitude of people in the West as commonplace truths.

(6) Even in Oxford and Cambridge, Indian students have often come to me and told me about their own difficulty in answering arguments used by their fellow students concerning Indian morals, which have been based on statements made in this continuous series of writings which have no object in view except to degrade India in the eyes of the West.

We cannot simply ignore all this that is going on openly under our very eyes—often with political motives behind it. To do so would be very foolish indeed. There must be provided some simple antidote against these deliberate assaults upon the fair name and honour of India which we are bound to defend.

"We want," the Indian students have said to me with touching earnestness, "a short and convincing answer put into our hands which we can show to our friends: for we know that the charges now being made are exaggerated and unfair, but we do not know how to contradict them. Cannot you yourself, who know India almost better than we do, write such a book, so that we may give it to our friends to read?"

Considerations such as these have made me take up the task at last, however late in the day. In doing so I have looked back at the notes which I put down long ago, and also at some articles published in Mahatma Gandhi's weekly paper, *Young India*, which received his own valuable scrutiny. By a bad mistake at the time they were only published in India. Among these I have found some of the material which I needed for the present book. But everything has been revised and much more has been added besides, so that this volume represents in a brief and simple form a constructive reply to this kind of attack on Indian moral character which has continued for several years.

It is true, of course, that the evil already done can never be wholly undone: we can never retrieve the past. But it is often possible to remove false impressions which have just been formed, and when an occasion arises it is surely our duty to do so. There is no danger of increasing the evil, which has been already committed, merely by reviving the subject; for the worst sensation, with all its bitterness, is over. To put the matter concisely, the continual asseveration of these charges against India, which have appeared without any serious contradiction, has made even those who desire to know the truth begin to believe that no answer is possible. This false idea must at all costs be removed, and a true idea of India must be given instead.

For the truth is that the moral foundation of Indian society, which can be traced in all Indian culture and civilization, remains stable and secure through the ages. It rests upon the immemorial village tradition, which is one of the permanent things in a world of constant change. It is this basis which those who have criticized India so harshly from the outside have never taken the trouble to understand.

One argument has been brought forward by those who have defended this kind of sensational literature which may be dismissed at once. It is asserted that, in spite of all its gross exaggeration, such writings have performed a public service by forcing the attention of the world upon some deep-seated evils in Hindu life. In this connexion an analogy has been drawn between *Mother India* and *Uncle Tom's Cabin*. For the latter book, it is stated, though giving a one-sided picture of the old slave days in the Southern States, dealt a mortal blow at the cruel wrong of slavery itself. It has even been suggested that the passing of the Sarda Act, raising the age of marriage in India, was indirectly due to the storm of protest aroused by *Mother India* throughout the whole civilized world.

But the two examples are not analogous. For Miss Mayo's experience of India was shallow. She was writing about a foreign country in which she had spent only a few months. Mrs. Harriet Beecher Stowe, on the other hand, was born in the United States and had lived there all her life. She had the right to speak out. Furthermore, later history has shown that where the picture drawn in *Uncle Tom's Cabin* was highly exaggerated it did mischief. The wound inflicted on the Southern States has not yet been fully healed.

While I have been writing I have taken my examples chiefly from *Mother India*, because it has had a world-wide circulation. It has thus become the head and front of all the offending. But my wish has been to go farther, and to help those who have not even heard Miss Mayo's name to understand and love India better. Nothing can be more important at the present time than intelligent appreciation and understanding. We have had far too much contempt in the West for races that are different from our own. Conquest and domination have created a "colour prejudice" which goes far deeper down into our subconsciousness than we are wont to imagine. We may not, as educated people, hold its cruder forms of stupid arrogance and vulgar abuse, but we should be very unwise if we regarded ourselves as rising altogether above it. Yet the subtle mischief, which this one-sided condemnation of India has often done, has been to stir up within us this superiority complex and rekindle it into a flame; and this has happened just at a time when the one way forward to sanity in human affairs is to determine that as we would wish the East to appreciate us, so ought we to seek with all our hearts to appreciate the East. Surely this is the Golden Rule which alone can bring back a genuine peace to mankind.

Let me repeat once more the thought that I have expressed in the Preface. The world in our own generation appears to be sinking back into the chaos of bitter hatred and party strife. It is a time, therefore, when every single word of good-will between the nations sincerely uttered may be of priceless value. The time is short and the odds against us are great. But the truth is on our side, and in the end it will prevail.

Chapter 1

THE ACCUSATION

The one theme which all these recent sensational volumes on India have set out to prove is that the Hindu religion, both by its ritual and practice, is a morally debasing faith.

Hinduism, they assert, lays such stress on sexual indulgence, and is so bound up with phallic worship in its grossest forms, that the vigour of the Hindu community has become altogether sapped and undermined. The picture of a society sunk in rottenness and obscenity is drawn in lurid colours and illustrated from the carvings of Hindu temples. This sexual viciousness is supposed to be produced wholly by religion and to have eaten into the virile life of the people, debilitating its manhood. The centre of all the mischief—so these books tell the West—is the moral debasement of the Hindu faith itself. One of these books goes so far as to represent Hinduism, not as a religion, but as a disease.

I shall speak plainly and openly, as this book goes on, about certain evils which have crept into Hinduism during the time of its decay and are still to be met with. Every ancient religion has its ages of vigorous growth and also its ages of decline. It is indisputable that more than a century ago, in the days of Raja Ram Mohan Roy, the decay of ancient Hinduism had become almost complete. "Ram

Mohan," writes Tagore, "was born at a time when our country, having lost its link with the inmost truths of its being, struggled under a crushing load of unreason, in abject slavery to circumstance. We had entered the zone of uncreative habit, of decadent tradition, and ceased to exercise our humanity."

"There are noble strains in Hindu thought," writes Edward Thompson in his historical chapter on Racial Estrangement, "and India has never lacked saints and mystics; but Hinduism was passing through a most unhappy phase and countenanced a multitude of revolting practices."[1] He goes on to show, as Tagore has done, the supreme greatness of Raja Ram Mohan Roy as he stood out against the hateful practice of widow burning and other evils in Hinduism hardly less revolting at that time.

These two verdicts, however severe, can be proved to be in accordance with indisputable historic facts. Christendom in the age of Pope Alexander VI and Caesar Borgia was wicked beyond all human belief, and countenanced such utterly revolting customs as the burning alive of innocent people as witches and the hideous tortures of the Inquisition. But just as the Christian Church underwent a reformation, so Hinduism to-day, owing to its great powers of revival, is reforming itself from within. It is therefore cruel beyond words to fasten upon it, just in this

[1] *Rise and Fulfilment of British Rule in India*, by Thompson and Garratt (Macmillan), p. 308 (second edition).

period of revival and reform, all the crudities of a bygone age.

While it would be quite easy to quote at length from the book called *Mother India* gross misrepresentations of modern Hinduism, I shall take instead, for the purpose of this chapter, some passages from a volume more recently published by Patricia Kendall, who has evidently tried to follow closely in the footsteps of Miss Mayo herself. She brought out, in an expensive form, both in Britain and America, a book called *India and the British: A Quest for Truth*. This volume she has dared to dedicate "To India: for the Truth can make her Free," as though her one object was to express sympathy with the Indian people. At the time of its publication, we are told, the demand for it by the reading public was so great that circulating libraries asked for it to be returned with all possible speed in order to supply a waiting list of members who desired to read it.

The one feature of the book, which evidently attracted attention and increased its sale, was a coarse description of Hinduism and its ritual-marks. These proved Hinduism, according to the author, to be a phallic and obscene religion.

The explanation of these symbols, which she had discovered in Hinduism, is put in the mouth of an imaginary missionary doctor, who informs an innocent young girl from the West about the facts.

"To cut through to the truth," asserts this woman doctor, Hinduism "is a social disease. It is a worship of elements, of natural features and forces, of deified men and animals, even of weapons and primitive implements, but principally of the powers of life, the organs of sex . . . only in Hinduism is degeneracy deified. The teachings and not just the interpretations of Hinduism sink to such depths that decent and proper words cannot correctly describe their level."

The same grotesque travesty of Hinduism is carried on in different parts of the book. Perhaps the worst passage of all is where the doctor is made to describe the marks, which orthodox Hindus place on their foreheads, in the following manner to the young girl whom she is instructing:—

"Every Hindu," she states, "bears upon his forehead, and on other parts of his body, the symbol of his particular deity and wears that symbol in amulets and bracelets and pieces of stone. The symbol of Siva is the phallus, which is called the *lingam*, and it is the lingam that is painted on his forehead and worn upon his person. The followers of Vishnu paint the female counterpart on their foreheads; it is called the *namam*. . . . These obscene emblems are as sacred to the Hindus as the Cross is to the Christians."

At this point, the author tells us, the young girl listener interrupted the woman doctor. She looked "rather sick and a little nauseated."

"Then Hindu religion is phallicism!"

"Yes," replied the doctor missionary. "It is exactly that, and that is what I meant when I said that Hinduism is a social disease. You may be able to visualize, to a comparatively small degree, the rituals and results of this creed. . . ."

"I don't want to see the Temple to-morrow," said the young girl. "It's all too disgusting."

"I advise you to go," the doctor answered. "You must see some Hindu temple, for how else can you change that disgust into pity? Isn't it a pitiful thing that these wonderful peoples have never been able to create a belief in a Divine and Righteous Being, exterior to and above themselves, to whom they can aspire and pay spiritual homage? . . . The Jaggannuth Temple here isn't so bad after all. The carvings aren't nearly so obscene as those at Madura, for Aurangzeb, the Mohammedan Emperor, called 'the Iconoclast,' mutilated many of the vilest depictions. By all means go."

It is necessary to pause at this point in order to make clear that Patricia Kendall's explanation of the caste marks which orthodox Hindus make on their foreheads is erroneous, and would not be accepted as accurate by any Hindu whom I have ever known. Furthermore, the phallic symbol that is so often found in the temples and in the village shrines has lost its primitive significance. Dr. J Bissett Pratt, in his book called *India and its Faiths*, thus writes about it:—

"Its exact origin is quite lost in antiquity: but phallic symbols are common all over the world, and this one seems to have been assimilated to the worship of Siva when the relatively uncultured people were admitted into Hinduism. . . . The *lingam* has, for nearly all Siva's worshippers, quite lost all sexual significance, and is simply the object in which Mahadev, the Great God, chooses to incarnate himself for the purposes of worship."

The same distortion of Hinduism in this book of Patricia Kendall's goes on page after page, and her ignorance at times would be ridiculous if it were not so desperately tragic in its depths of misunderstanding. The name of Mahatma Gandhi rouses her scorn. But her greatest contempt is reserved for the Hindu religion itself, and here she shows no mercy and no imagination.

Those of us who have lived long among the Hindus, as this author has never done, and have witnessed the deep sincerity of their daily religious life, especially that of the women of the household, can do nothing but writhe at the insults which she pours upon the Hindu faith as though it were one of the most obscene things on the earth. An insult to what one holds to be sacred, such as Patricia Kendall continually repeats, is like an injury against one's own mother. Those who know and love India best feel the wound of the insult most deeply. Her object seems to be to exalt the special virtues of the British. She tries to do this in such a way as to afford to a certain type of English man or woman a secret satisfaction at the contrast with his own ideals and make him say within himself, like the Pharisee of old, "God, I thank Thee that I am not as other men are, or even as this Hindu!"

An Australian, who had lived among the people of India as an artist for three and a half years and had learnt to admire them, wrote in the *Amrita Bazar Patrika* as follows:—

"I am merely an artist, a reciter of verse, with only the most superficial and scanty knowledge of these great subjects. I have said that I know nothing of the Hindu religion. It is true. But this I do know: that if Hinduism is the foundation of their toleration of other religions; if it is the foundation of their great and glorious culture; of their remarkable ability to appreciate and absorb the culture of the West, while losing none of their own; of the loving courtesy and hospitality which they have extended to me, an Australian, throughout the length and breadth of this great country, then that religion must be a thing of beauty and a vivifying power."

It has been necessary thus to express the indignation which arises when such a cruel travesty of Hinduism is set forward with an air of racial superiority in the name of Truth. What follows in these pages will serve to show, by many personal examples and experiences, that Patricia Kendall, instead of representing by her book the "Truth," has given her readers nothing but a painfully distorted impression. She has spread abroad by such writing a one-sided picture of India and Hindu religion which can only leave behind a bitter sense of injustice.

A typical Hindu writer, N. N. Chowdhury, has the following comment, which by its fairness and courtesy puts such writers to shame:—

"The beauty of Christianity lies in its conception

of brotherly love. 'This is My Commandment,' says Jesus Christ, 'that ye love one another as I have loved you. . . . Greater love hath no man than this that a man lay down his life for his friends.' Had these commandments been adhered to, the Kingdom of God would have been a reality long ago. But to-day the foremost Christian nations of the West do not seem to abide by the precepts of Jesus: not love, but intolerance, antagonism, and hatred are being deliberately fostered in an appeal to philanthropy, social work, and world welfare."

I have shown Patricia Kendall's remarks concerning the caste marks on the foreheads of devout worshippers to the highest Sanskrit authority within our Asram, at Santiniketan, who has an intimate knowledge of the Hinduism of village India to-day as well as of all the records of the past. He has assured me that whatever may have been their origin in a remote and obscure age long ago, they have now absolutely no significance of the kind that Patricia Kendall mentions, nor do the Hindus themselves associate the ideas of phallicism with their worship of Mahadeva—as Shiva is usually called.

If primitive origins are searched and tabulated all over the world, it can easily be shown that phallic symbolism underlies many of the most ancient and hallowed customs in the West as well as in the East. For at one early stage in human history it was spread far and wide. But when we use those ancient customs or symbols to-day, we do not associate them with sex. For they have lost all that primitive meaning. The same is true of India.

I shall return to this point in a later chapter, and further evidence will there be provided against the theory that these marks have a sexual origin and are associated with sex ideas at the present time. No one who has lived for a long while in India and come to understand the Hindu religious ideals could dream of sexual imagery being now connected with these ritual marks. Most Hindu scholars would deny that they ever had any such connexion.

It is quite impossible to go into detail at this point concerning other misstatements of a similar character which appear in Patricia Kendall's book. But the specimen, with which I have dealt here at considerable length, will show how unreliable the information is which is thus being spread all over the world concerning the Hindu religion.

NOTE

Mahatma Gandhi writes with regard to similar accusations in *Mother India* as follows:—

"She says that the Vaishnava mark has an obscene meaning. I am a born Vaishnavite. I have perfect recollection of my visits to Vaishnava temples. Mine were orthodox people. I used to have the mark myself as a child, but neither I, nor any one else in our family, ever knew that this harmless and rather elegant-looking mark had any obscene significance at all. I asked a party of Vaishnavites in Madras. They knew nothing about the alleged obscene significance. I therefore suggest that millions are unaware of the obscenity alleged to be behind it. It has remained for our Western visitors to acquaint us with the obscenity of many practices which we have hitherto innocently indulged in."

Chapter 2

GLARING MISSTATEMENTS

It is necessary to make clear by a second conspicuous example how entirely inaccurate and ill-informed are the criticisms which are now being brought forward, not merely about Hinduism as a religion, but also concerning Indian life. These have often the appearance of being well documented, but their inaccuracy can easily be demonstrated by those who know the facts. Unfortunately, such knowledge is not always ready to hand. It is also quite impossible to expose each one of them where the number is so great.

I have taken in this chapter a typical example of Miss Mayo's inaccuracies, where she criticizes one who is peculiarly well known to me, namely, the poet, Rabindranath Tagore. For he is my own deeply revered friend, with whom I have lived in closest touch for over a quarter of a century. It is therefore easy for me to check her statements about him.

In order to make clear the extremely offensive character of this attack, I must first of all explain Tagore's own reputation in India as a champion of social reform. He stands out head and shoulders above his contemporaries, not only as a poet, musician, and artist, but also as a "modern" in all social matters who fearlessly and openly carries out in practice what he advocates in his writings. He is in direct spiritual succession from the greatest of modern Indian leaders, Raja Ram Mohan Roy. He cherishes all that reformer's ideals, seeking to make them his own. A more utterly courageous worker in the highest humanitarian causes could scarcely be found.

One great event in each calendar year has been always looked forward to with eagerness in Calcutta. It is Rabindranath Tagore's Bengali message at the Ram Mohan Roy Anniversary. On such occasions he has never failed to point his country forward in the direction of social progress on modern scientific lines, while preserving all that is good in India's ancient traditions. Though a poet, he can be amazingly practical. This attitude of Tagore, as an advanced thinker and worker, is well known throughout the length and breadth of India. Indeed, he has suffered greatly, and has even been excommunicated on this account by orthodox Brahmins in Bengal.

In his institution near Calcutta, called Santiniketan, Tagore has built up a home of liberal education on modern idealist lines, where Indian girls in ever-increasing numbers come for their higher studies and live a free and healthy life. He has thus aimed, not only by his writings but also by his actions, during nearly half a century, at raising the age of marriage; and the recent Sarda Marriage Act owes not a little to his persistent advocacy of that reform over this long period. Here again his acts have told even more than his words. I have been very closely associated with Santiniketan during the greater part of my life in India, so that I can write with authority on this subject. Every part of the work that Tagore has built up with such marked perseverance is thoroughly familiar to me.

Equally in the matter of medical help in the villages round his Asram, Tagore has always been an ardent social worker. His efforts at Santiniketan in this respect have won the high regard of different members of the Rockefeller Foundation who have come to visit and inspect what he has been able to accomplish. One of their doctors who lived with me in the Asram for some time praised the work whole-heartedly after a thorough examination. He was enthusiastic about it in all his long talks with me before his departure.

A brilliant American doctor, a Quaker, Dr. Harry Timbres, whom Tagore had gladly taken on his staff, has written as follows:—

"The health work has been organized in eight of the surrounding villages. I find that the claim of reducing the incidence of malaria in one village from 87 to 18 per cent approaches very close to the radical side of the truth, the spleen index in this village having been 25 per cent, and the general physical state of nourishment of the villagers being noticeably better than in other villages. It is all a splendid work being done along proper lines, without waste of effort, by young men whose ideals for their country are of the highest and whose patience in doing the necessary little things is infinite."

Here then is Tagore's record, both with regard to child marriage reform and also with regard to medical aid among the villages on Western lines. In both cases, what he has written in his books he has practised in his own life.

Yet with amazement we find that Miss Mayo, without even visiting his Asram (though it is within easy reach of Calcutta), has pilloried Tagore in her book on India as one who professes high principles in the West without practising them in his own country! She chooses the two questions of *child marriage* and *medical aid for the poor* as the two points where he has retarded Indian progress. What is even more astounding, she has attempted to do this in each case by a misquotation!

Let me explain this, so that the reader may understand by a signal example how unreliable these books are. As I said at the end of the last chapter, it is not possible to go through in detail all the multitude of errors with which this literature is studded, but one specimen may surely suffice. Here then is the way she misquotes.

Tagore had been asked by Count Keyserling to explain for Western readers the ancient Indian idea of marriage. He accepted the invitation and gave certain reasons why Indians in the past had encouraged early marriage. He wrote as follows:—

"There is a particular age, said India, at which this attraction between the sexes reaches its height: so if marriage is to be regulated according to the social will (as distinguished from the choice of the individual concerned) it must be finished with before such age. Hence the Indian custom of early marriage."

When Miss Mayo quoted this passage she omitted the two words "said India" in the first sentence and placed dots there instead. In this way she presented the passage as giving Tagore's own ideas concerning child marriage, though he had expressly written the two words "said India" in his text. That is to say, by omitting these two words she left her readers to understand that this was Tagore's own theory and that he had acted upon it, while the truth is the very reverse of this. Only when the reviewers had discovered her literary offence and verified Tagore's sentence in Count Keyserling's book did she insert these two words "said India" in her text. To complete the offence she based her accusation of hypocrisy, which she levelled against Tagore, upon them.

Her ignorance of India may be judged from the fact that she was not even aware that every educated Indian knows well Tagore's lifelong opposition to and condemnation of child marriage. Indians realise equally well that he is one of the greatest living social reformers in the whole of India.

The second passage in her book relating to Tagore is even more misleading. She charges the Indian poet, as an intellectual, with holding antiquated *medical* views, equivalent to "voodoo" doctoring among the bush negroes of the West Indies. Her words are as follows:—

"With the Indian National Congress claiming

that aruvedic [*sic*] medicine is 'just as scientific as modern Western medicine,' with such men as Sir Rabindranath Tagore, the poet, fervently declaring that aruvedic science surpasses anything that the West can offer, and with Swarajists in general pushing it forward on patriotic grounds, you get the melancholy spectacle of the meagre appropriations allotted to medicine and public health in this most disease-stricken of lands being heavily cut to perpetuate a science on the same level as 'voodoo' doctoring of the West Indian negro."

In the English editions of *Mother India* the index contains, at this reference, the words "Tagore quoted." During an interview, when I challenged her to produce this quotation from any of Tagore's writings, she confessed to me that she had none to offer, and told me that the index had not been drawn up by herself. She then went on to state that some one, whose name she would not give me, had *told* her that Rabindranath Tagore had expressed such a view!

So then, on this second-hand, hearsay information in a book which professes to be carefully documented, she had published this libellous statement. She has pointedly informed her large reading public in edition after edition of *Mother India* that Tagore had "fervently declared" that the Ayurvedic[1] system

[1] Her own ignorance of this system is so great that she did not even know how to *spell* the word! She had spelt it in all the earlier editions "aruvedic," which makes nonsense. Again, she is unaware that to put this highly developed medical system of ancient India on a level with "voodoo" doctoring is to display her own ignorance in all Indian eyes.

of ancient Indian medicine (which she puts on the same level as "voodoo" doctoring) "surpasses anything the West can offer"!

In spite of the fact that Tagore himself had denounced this statement of hers as a pure falsehood and had challenged her to give her reference; in spite of the fact, which every one in India knows, that Tagore employs modern medical Western science with all its latest discoveries in his own institution at Santiniketan, which she never visited; in spite of his reputation throughout Bengal as one of the keenest promoters of research work in malaria prevention along modern Western lines, she had continued to reprint this libel. Only the great reluctance of Tagore to take the whole matter into the courts of law stood in the way of an action for libel being filed. The original wrong done to a very noble poet and philosopher, whom India reveres, was all the more serious because these words, which he never uttered and never *could* have uttered, have been reproduced both in England and America and have been circulated all over the world. When challenged, as I have related, to bring forward a single line written by him which would bear out her accusation, she has failed to do so.

It has been well worth while thus entering into full detail with regard to this special inaccuracy, because it is impossible for the ordinary reader to check statements which are said to be "well documented," and one is apt to take for granted that they have been verified by the author before publication.

I have now almost completed thirty-five years in the East, living all the while in closest contact with Indians themselves and sharing in a very great measure their domestic and social life. Above all, I can speak of the villages; for my wanderings up and down India, especially in times of distress, have brought me very near to the village people. They have learnt to know me and to love me as their personal friend, and have admitted me into their confidence. The kindness that I have received at their hands has been unspeakably great. They have never concealed from me for one moment things that have been evil in their social life and practice. They have always been most outspoken.

Since I have been called in time after time to help in seasons of distress, such as flood and famine and pestilence, I have constantly witnessed the darker side of this village life as well as its nobler side of sacrifice. Also I have learnt to understand the very precarious and pitifully poverty-stricken conditions under which a vast number of them live. With outward circumstances so much against them, it has been a continual wonder to me that their standards of life have remained so high and that adversity has not dragged them down to a lower level. The one thing that I can assert with positive assurance, after all this intimate experience, is that Western writers such as I have quoted are entirely on the wrong track when they put down India's misery and poverty to extravagant sexual indulgence. I hope to show that such a theory is based on a misrepresentation of the facts similar to that which I have tried to expose in these two opening chapters. In what follows I shall deal mainly with the larger issues and try to explain what is *really* happening in India before our eyes if we will have patience to study the subject.

NOTE

It might possibly be argued that the serious misquotations of Tagore in *Mother India* are an exceptional case. So far, however, from their being exceptional, I have met others whom the authoress has misrepresented in the same inaccurate manner. In Appendix I and II rejoinders will be found briefly reproduced. Others of a similar character have been published by Mrs. K. C. Roy and Lord Sinha. Miss K. M. Bose of Lahore was also greatly distressed at the garbled account of an interview given by her, which is related in *Mother India*, and the Head of Dayal Bagh, near Agra, Sahebji Maharaj, told me personally that he had been terribly upset by the way in which he himself had been misreported. Sentences were put in his mouth, he said, as having been uttered by him, which he would never have dreamt of using. The same desire to make a sensational statement by exaggeration runs all through this kind of literature.

Chapter 3

THE NATIONAL AWAKENING

PERHAPS the most searching test of any book which sets out to condemn the home life and character of another people is to examine how far the author has been able to discern the vital spiritual forces that are at work beneath the surface of society. For these are always the main factor in the cleansing process that purges away old abuses. Every country needs this cleansing: Great Britain and America have many crying evils still unremedied. The sovereign test is to examine how far the new forces have been able to break through the old routine and perform their purifying work. Wherever that has been made possible a national awakening has already begun.

With remarkable unanimity those who are competent to judge have pointed out that India is singularly fortunate to-day in possessing such restorative forces working from within outwards. Yet a whole series of writers, who have written recently about India's moral decadence, have missed these favourable signs altogether. The fashion was set by *Mother India*, which was in this respect the worst offender. The authoress went further still in a later book called *The Slaves of the Gods*.[1] There she has poured utter scorn on the national movement itself and on those who are working under Mahatma

[1] See for a glaring example of this, Appendix III, p. 244.

Gandhi. She also betrays evidence that her information must have been largely taken from that isolated band of foreigners who know little about India.

It is easy to trace to this narrow coterie the different stories, which she relates with such gusto, about the Bengalis, whom she has obviously been taught to dislike; how "not a virgin or a rupee" would be left in Bengal if the military races from the north are allowed to have their own way. In every instance she echoes what may be called the "European Club" point of view. The distortion of truth which these pictures represent would have caused the book to be thrown aside in disgust and forgotten by Indians themselves, if she had not transgressed all bounds of decency and attacked both the religion and the domestic moral character of those who are rightly held most dear. It is this that took the volume at once out of the class of hastily composed and foolishly omniscient writings, and made it an insult and a humiliation.

One of the most serious offences in this type of propaganda is that it takes every opportunity of depreciating Mahatma Gandhi himself, whose character in India is revered by every Indian, just as Washington and Lincoln are revered in America. It also seeks to belittle the moral success which he has achieved. During the non-co-operation movement he had called himself a "rebel"—albeit a non-violent one. He dared to challenge the Government of India itself, a thing which Miss Mayo and others never forgive. For she appears to belong to that peculiar class in the Eastern States of America which upholds the British Empire at all costs and defends everything that it has done as though it were sacrosanct. Her partisanship in these matters is more "British" than that of the British themselves, and often highly embarrassing.

Thus she remains fixed and rooted to the one idea that the only people who are doing honest and serious work to remedy India's age-long evil customs are the officials and the missionaries, along with a few entirely anglicized Indians who are working under them and have lost touch with their own national movement. She does not realize that these very officials would be the first to tell her that their labour is altogether lost unless Indian villagers themselves take the initiative, and not only commence to reform their villages, but also carry through those reforms. For it is nothing more than a "treadmill" existence, where as soon as the official pressure is relaxed things immediately fall back into the old rut. District officers themselves have told me that their work is never complete until it results in a movement among the people to carry it forward. They also know quite well that they, as foreigners, have not got the persuasive power to create a truly popular movement.

Now it so happens that in recent years the masses of the villagers have been roused in a manner that had never happened before for centuries past. The national awakening of the masses has carried all before it. Old abuses, such as the increasing consumption of alcohol and opium, seem to have vanished almost in a night. To take a single instance: Mahatma Gandhi visited Assam, where the opium addiction was at its worst, and in six months the consumption was reduced by more than one-third owing mainly to his personal influence and moral weight of persuasion. What is more, the rate of consumption has never gone up again, but has gradually become still further reduced. Miracles such as this have been happening every day. Untouchability during these wonderful years has received its deadliest blow. Social reforms have been advancing from strength to strength.

But non-co-operation, according to the officials whom Miss Mayo visited at the time, implied a "revolt" against British rule. Therefore she has nothing but condemnation for it, and also for those who took part in it, especially Mahatma Gandhi. She definitely takes sides against him.

Yet in these times through which India has been passing, with all their turmoil and upheaval, it is easy to note how a great dynamic personality, such as that of Gandhi, has had inconceivably vaster power of moral appeal to remove social abuses than any mere act of legislation passed in the Central Assembly at New Delhi. For the lasting impression which he has been able to make upon the innermost life of India is due above all to the fact that what he commands the people to do does not depend on any external force, or material wealth, or worldly power, but on *soul* force alone. I have constantly talked with the villagers about this, and have invariably found that his moral character has been the one secret of his supreme personal attraction. He has become the very embodiment of their own idea of goodness. Indeed, to his great embarrassment, they often regard him as divine.

It is one of the most unaccountable things to me that all this national awakening which has been aroused by Mahatma Gandhi is hardly mentioned in *Mother India*, except for condemnation. I do not think that the author has merely slurred over in silence what she has seen. Her peculiar lack of insight seems rather to be due to the extremely hurried nature of her visit, and also to the class of persons from whom she received her information. In judging and weighing her standards of accuracy we have to remember that she wrote this book after a single cold weather tour, during which she appears to have occupied a large part of her time with visits paid to officials. She would therefore naturally tend to see things chiefly through their eyes and take their point of view.

There are to-day in India hard-working, capable, and self-sacrificing British officials, many of whom have a close touch with the people of the country and a knowledge of the deeper forces that are at work in modern India. But one of the saddest things that has happened in recent years, making reform long overdue, is the ever-widening gulf between the people and the administration, which revealed itself in a startling manner during the non-co-operation movement. When Miss Mayo determined to rely on official statements and the "European Club" point of view, she was actually courting disaster. For India has moved forward far beyond official tutelage, and the "club" opinion with regard to what is happening is prejudiced and narrow. It is true that she went to see Mr. Gandhi and a few other Indians of note, who were not likely to take a purely official view; but the number of these was small, and in almost every case the bitter complaint has since been raised that she has misrepresented their opinions. By far the most serious of all the errors that followed from this procedure was that both she and those who followed her became tempted to write contemptuously about Mahatma Gandhi himself and the remarkable work that he has accomplished. Nothing could give greater offence or do more to embitter mutual relations than sneering references to one whom every Indian regards with reverence on account of his life of utter self-sacrifice for the sake of his country.

Since these sensational books were written the value of Mahatma Gandhi's work as a man of truth and peace has been recognized by the British officials themselves, from the Viceroy downwards. Nothing is dreaded so much as the day when he may be obliged to retire from the scene. This fact should be sufficient to show how completely these writers have failed to judge for themselves the spiritual forces which are at work in India to-day, bringing about that reform from within which goes as deep as life itself.

For the full reform programme which Mahatma Gandhi has taken up, along with his devoted followers, includes every one of those main evils which have been so vehemently condemned, and all along the line there are amazing signs of progress. While dealing directly with these evils, Mahatma Gandhi's personal moral sway among the masses has reached wider and wider circles. I have gone out often to meet him on his tours and have lived with him in different parts of India. Wherever he has passed along the country-side his influence has been paramount and unique. He does not sit at ease in his "pleasant and comfortable home at Sabarmati," as *Mother India* has so contemptuously pictured him. Rather, he has undertaken the most difficult journeys throughout the length and breadth of India. These have often involved incredible hardship and suffering. Again and again his health and strength have broken down under almost impossible conditions. He has penetrated the most remote country districts, and has lived in the very midst of the "untouchables" almost as one of themselves.

This whole movement of social reform which he has thus started has been carried forward by eager men and women, who have caught the true spirit of their leader. In this way things which might have taken centuries to achieve are likely to be accomplished in a single generation. It would be hard to find a parallel to the moral influence of this one single personality over vast bodies of people, or a more heroic record of sacrifice on behalf of a great and noble cause.

What has truly amazed me as I have watched it has been to see young men and women, who have had great possessions, gladly changing their daily habits of luxury for a life of extreme hardship with the joy of new-found freedom. Such is Jawaharlal Nehru, the son of a famous lawyer, Pandit Motilal Nehru, who was among the wealthy men of India. The whole family sacrificed all that was dear on behalf of the national cause. Jawaharlal has suffered imprisonment again and again, along with hundreds and thousands of others who have offered no resistance.

To give another example, such was the young Muslim, Umar Sobhani, one of the richest men in Bombay, who gave up much of his worldly position and suffered great hardships which brought about an early death. Such again was C. R. Das, who abandoned the most lucrative practice at the Calcutta Bar and went through incredible difficulties and labours in spite of his ill-health till death intervened. Such again are Shankerlal Banker and Jamnalal Bajaj—but the list would be far too long to give in full. In every instance that I have mentioned a richer mode of living, with all its comforts and luxuries, has been left joyfully behind for simple fare, a dress of homespun (*khaddar*), and a life spent in continual sacrifice for their country's good. Side by side with these there have also been noble women who have played their part. To mention one name only, Kamala Nehru, the wife of Jawaharlal Nehru, literally sacrificed life itself for the cause. At one time, in the more recent passive resistance movement, the women took up the work and carried it on after the leaders on the men's side had suffered imprisonment.

Nor must it for a moment be thought that such sacrifices were made by the educated classes only. On the contrary, the greatest devotion of all has been shown by those who were poor. They have carried on the painful struggle to the very end. If it be argued that all this was a purely political matter, such a contention is not a true statement of the case, as I have already tried to show. No one who took active part in the national movement could keep up social distinctions, or even religious aloofness. The movement itself implied freedom from age-long social and religious abuses. Mahatma Gandhi had impressed on all his followers from the very first that the passive resistance offered must be pure.

I have often related the parable of the hand and wrist, whereby he has occasionally taught the village people how the whole movement must be conducted and what are its chief ingredients. The five fingers, he would suggest, represent the essential things without which India cannot receive her freedom. The first would be Hindu-Muslim unity; for no united India can be built up without that. The second would be the removal of "untouchability," which is equally necessary if India is to be one people. The middle finger would stand for equality between man and woman, for that is quite fundamental. On the other side of the centre there would be prohibition of the drug and liquor traffic which is ruining the morals of the people; and last of all would come the promotion of village industries, especially hand-spinning and hand-weaving. Then, as a uniting force, the wrist, which binds the five fingers of the hand together, stands for *Ahimsa*, or Non-violence, in thought and word and deed. For this *Ahimsa* is the soul-force which combines all the social and economic aspects of the one national programme together and makes it thus a living organized whole with a moral purpose behind it.

When such a schedule is examined it will easily be seen that moral factors predominate and separate it entirely from any ordinary political programme. Its end, indeed, is nothing less than the regeneration of the whole Indian people from within: and with Mahatma Gandhi it is deeds that count most. For no one is more severe than he is with regard to the hypocrisy of profession without practice.

If all these things are taken into consideration by a sympathetic observer the verdict is likely to be given that nowhere in the whole world are abuses and evils being swept so rapidly away as in India. It may also be fairly stated that in no country are the political ideals so high.

Chapter 4

THE NEW SPIRIT

THOSE men and women who, under Mahatma Gandhi's leadership, have joyfully gone to prison without offering any active resistance have surely won the right by their suffering and sacrifice to speak on behalf of their fellow countrymen and to rebut the charge which Miss Mayo and others have brought against them of being a morally decadent and sexually degraded race. Their own supreme devotion to their country has also given them the responsibility of interpreting the higher longings of all the countless, inarticulate folk in the seven hundred thousand villages of India. These poor people cannot speak for themselves, and are therefore unable to contradict the accusations that have been levelled against their moral character and their religion by hostile and sensational writers.

Hitherto I have spoken mainly about the men who have imbibed the new spirit. But the women also have been roused to action by the heroic example of Mahatma Gandhi and his brave wife, Kasturbai. The latter has been a fearless leader on behalf of the depressed classes, and also in the great cause of woman's emancipation from the bondage of social custom. The women keep aflame in a remarkable manner to-day the ardent spirit of sacrifice on behalf of their country which Mahatma Gandhi has kindled.

As soon as they show this spirit in action a place of honour is given to them in the hearts of the masses of the people. There is no more welcome change than this remarkable new leadership of women in all that exalts and uplifts India. By this means much more has been done to secure women's rights, to raise the age of marriage, to sweep away class distinctions, and to abolish the purdah system than has been carried out in the past in spite of many generations of heroic effort. All that earlier endeavour on the part of noble women, like Pandita Ramabai and others, has not been wasted. It is now at last coming to fruition.

In the chapters which follow much more will be written about this wonderful advance among the women; for on no side of modern Indian life has the change been so rapid and beneficial. I shall also have much to say about the heavy deadweight of evil custom which still remains to be removed.

One further side of the national movement may be taken, namely, the very remarkable and effective energy, directed towards social service, which has been shown in action by Indian Youth. Here I am able to write with first-hand knowledge of the facts, because I have been closely associated in India with enterprises undertaken by those who have rightly gained the name of "national volunteers."

There is one scene still fresh in my mind at Vaikom, in the Travancore State, where a struggle was carried on under the guidance of Mahatma Gandhi. It aimed at throwing open a high road running along the side of a famous Hindu temple. This road had been exclusively occupied by Brahmins, who would not allow any member of the Scheduled Castes, whom they regarded as "untouchable," from setting foot on it. They regarded themselves and the temple as polluted if this should happen. The suffering caused by this cruelly selfish conduct was very great, because in monsoon weather this high road was the only means of passing from one part of the country to the other.

Mr. George Joseph, an Indian Christian barrister, started the campaign for opening the road. He went through the Brahmin quarter accompanied by a member of the depressed classes. Both of them were severely beaten by the Brahmins; and when they persisted in going forward the police intervened and placed them in custody on the charge of trespassing and breaking the peace.

At once hundreds of volunteers came forward to offer passive resistance in the same manner. But when a large number had been imprisoned by the Travancore State the police were ordered not to arrest any more, but to guard the road and prevent anyone by force from trespassing on it.

Then Mahatma Gandhi told the volunteers to stand opposite the police day by day in an attitude of prayer, with hands upraised, pleading silently for the right to go along the public highway. Each morning, therefore, after prayers the volunteers marched from their camp and set themselves opposite the police with folded hands. After standing thus for three hours a relief guard came on duty, and so it went on all through the day. But only when more than a year of this silent non-violent resistance had elapsed was there any desire on the part of the Brahmins to come to terms.

What moved the people of India most of all was to read in the newspapers how, in spite of the road being flooded waist-deep in water during the worst part of the monsoon, these young men never gave way. The police were allowed to moor a boat across the water, fixed with ropes, and thus to stand on guard dry-shod: but the volunteers were ready to remain opposite them hour after hour in the flood during the whole time of their "watch and ward." When I went down, at Mahatma Gandhi's request, to visit them and remain with them for a time, I was very deeply touched by their heroic conduct. When I went in the evening to visit the Brahmins and to plead with them, I found them still angry and abusive.

But gradually a change came over them, and after a season they relented. At last, with their full consent, the road was thrown open and the moral victory was won.

There can be no doubt that this great victory of non-violence did more than anything else to bring about a new attitude towards the millions of depressed humanity in South India, about which much will be told in a later chapter. Here I would only point out that young volunteers, who could carry through unflinchingly such a campaign as that, reveal a new spirit in India which can sweep away all kinds of evils and abuses. They would be an honour to any country.

This younger generation has thus brought a religious spirit into national work, preserving the devotion and worship that have been the strength of India in bygone days. The same spirit is helping to bring about emancipation from many of the evil customs that have grown up in the past and separated man from man. It is in keeping with the whole trend of the Youth Movement in India to-day.

One last example may be given of the power of this Youth Movement, which also came under my own observation, so that I can write about it with first-hand knowledge of the facts. In Orissa the greatest misery of all exists among the very poor, who are attached to the soil. A large proportion of these cultivators come from the "depressed classes." For in that province untouchability has become a standing disgrace which needs to be wiped out by those who have received the new spirit of brotherhood from Mahatma Gandhi. This degradation of man has crushed the people so cruelly that their misery has become chronic. Increasing addiction to opium has been the last refuge of the wretched. Constant floods, which may sweep away the crops of a whole year in a single night, add greatly to the spiritual depression and also to the spread of physical disease. Owing to the very rapid rise of the Mahanadi River at the height of the monsoon, these floods are almost yearly expected in the delta, and they are looked forward to with dread.

Late in the year 1927 (to give this single instance) eighty thousand houses were washed away. The national workers, who immediately came to the rescue, differed widely in caste and religion and social rank; but as volunteers, rescuing their fellow men and women from a cruel fate, they were all one brotherhood together. They went out into the midst of the floods, risking their lives not only from death by drowning, but also from pestilence, in one of the most malignantly malarial parts of India. Fever was at its worst at that time, and protection from it least available. Women helped in this work of relief as well as men. The very generous gifts that were sent from all parts of India united every province in face of a common disaster.

The people of Orissa at first were helpless in their despondency: but as soon as these young national volunteers arrived their courage revived. In the midst of all this the word was passed round that Mahatma Gandhi was coming to their rescue. Immediately hope was restored. Though he was very ill when he came, the poor half-starved people were permitted to flock round him and get what comfort they could from his presence.

Scenes like those I have described are frequently occurring, and their effect is manifest among the people. Changes and upheavals, amounting to nothing less than a social and moral revolution, are happening before our eyes. The wrongs of untouchability; the evils of child marriage; the insanitation; the baneful purdah system; the injustice of enforced widowhood—all these and a thousand other evils are being broken down from within. *But there is hardly a single mention of this in these books which condemn the Indian people wholesale as physically and morally degraded.*

The buttresses of conservative habit may still look very imposing from the outside and the walls of orthodoxy may yet appear to be strong; but the inner fortress of the human will has already been invaded and its capture is certain. The new reforms which Mahatma Gandhi has initiated will be all the more lasting because they have touched the hearts of the people themselves and are being carried out by their own effort.

There is a time when the warm weather comes, in the higher ranges of the Himalayas, that is known to all travellers in those remote regions. A vast mass of snow will seem to be eternally fixed upon the mountain-side by its icy grip on the rocks which lie beneath. For weeks during the first days of summer there appears no outward change, though all the while the grip upon the rocks is being loosened by the warm glow of the sun. Then the avalanche begins, and in a short space of time the whole mass of snow disappears.

In the same way, these hoary customs of ancient India, which seem so firmly established, are beginning to feel the warm glow of the sunshine of a new age. For the moment they still appear to be firmly fixed, but when once the avalanche begins they will surely disappear.

A story told by Dr. Rajan, Minister for Public Health in the Madras Government, may here be recorded. The Minister stated that Mahatma Gandhi had prevented his own life from becoming a wreck in earlier years when he was at college. For in those younger days he had become "the perfect rebel and iconoclast," discontented with the restriction of his environment and position. But he chanced to come in contact with Mahatma Gandhi, who had just then arrived from South Africa. He had the privilege of spending many hours one night in Mr. Gandhi's company, and this proved the turning-point in his own life. For he owed to that inspiring contact with a saint the softening of his heart and the changing of his spiritual vision.

Chapter 5

VILLAGE INDIA

A CONSTRUCTIVE picture is needed in order to show what Indian domestic life really is, and how wrong is the portrait offered to Western readers by Patricia Kendall and others. It is clearly not sufficient to counteract the mischief by a mere negative, denying the charges which have been brought forward. Something affirmative is required.

The vast bulk of the people of India (numbering about 90 per cent of the whole) live in villages and small hamlets, not in great cities. Large towns are singularly rare, and many of them are of recent growth: but these village people, for the most part, are remote from town life. Where no railway is near at hand this remoteness at times amounts almost to complete isolation.

The village social structure makes up on every side the one all-pervading background of India, ancient and modern. To a peculiar degree it represents Mother India herself. For India does not mean the large modern cities like Calcutta and Bombay.

This village life has also got a character and vitality of its own, which should be studied with very sensitive and delicate care if its inner secret is to be discovered. A study of this kind cannot possibly be undertaken in a hurry! It requires the most patient research.

Such a primary fact about India evidently came home at an early stage to Miss Mayo herself, and she writes as follows:—

"Villages—villages—villages—the true homes of India, scattered, miles apart, across the open country. Each just a handful of mud-walled huts, clustered beside the hole they took the mud from, now half full of stagnant water, in which they wash and bathe and quench their thirst. In villages such as these lives nine-tenths of all the people of India."

A description like this shows us that she had been at least able to grasp this one patently obvious fact that India is agricultural to the core. But having grasped this, it becomes all the more inexcusable that she and others also have gone on to generalize about the vicious character of Indian manhood by taking from the city areas figures with regard to diseases caused by sexual vice. They could not possibly be true of Indian village life, and are of doubtful correctness even about the towns.

Since India, as we have just seen, is essentially a land of villages, it follows that the morals of India are in the long run practically equivalent to the *morals which prevail in the country rather than in the towns*. If the village life is altogether rotten, then India must be rotten. But if this village life is still healthy, then the moral life of India must be healthy.

My own conviction, after an experience of over thirty years, is this: that though there may be many serious evils which have to be overcome, and bad customs which have still to be changed for something better, the village life of India as a whole is normally free from the grosser forms of sexual vice which Miss Mayo so luridly depicts.

Where there are in all more than seven hundred and fifty thousand villages, each with a character of its own, only a long and intimate residence in India on the part of a foreigner, together with a knowledge of the language, can give experience sufficient to state with confidence that the main facts have been ascertained. This village life is so varied that most of us, even those who have stayed longest in the country, grow less confident about the things we had once believed to be true.

There is a remarkably able book by an American lady, Miss Gertrude Emerson, called *Voiceless India.*[1] She has been one of the most brilliant of the research workers who have visited India from the West. The evils of Indian village life have been faithfully pointed out by her as well as all that is good. But no Indian has resented for a moment the damaging things that she has said, because before writing her book she spent more than a year in a single village learning to make friends with the people and to share their hard lot with them. Indeed, since writing her book, she has given up her whole life to India. When I showed her book to the poet, Rabindranath Tagore, he was so fascinated with it that he could hardly stop reading it till he had come to the last chapter. Here then is one who has a *claim* to write

[1] George Allen & Unwin, Ltd.

a book on Village India. But what claim can writers possess who have been casual visitors only, and have suffered none of the hardships of Indian life as it is really lived by great masses of the people?

Certain characteristics stand out in Village India with clearness and distinction. In no country in the world, for instance, are acts of criminal violence less frequent than in these villages taken as a whole; yet sexual vice is widely recognized as a potent cause of violent deeds of crime. This ought to have put Miss Mayo, as an enquirer, on her guard against making hasty assumptions.

Crime of any kind is singularly rare. Drunkenness is rare also, except in some of the toddy-drinking areas of the south, and also in parts of the north. Opium—the curse of China—is hardly a curse in India, even though it can be openly bought at any licensed shop. There are a few black spots, chiefly in the towns. Also in the two provinces of Assam and Orissa opium consumption is excessive, but not elsewhere.

Animal life is not slaughtered for daily food over the greater part of the country as far as Hindus are concerned. Coarse kinds of grain—chiefly rice, millet, and pulse—form the staple diet. Wheat takes the place of rice in the north. The poverty is extreme. Only the barest necessities are ever purchased with money. The whole atmosphere of the village is incredibly bare and simple. All this represents an abstemious life which is far removed from indulgence in vicious practice. The conditions are terribly hard, and life is lived away from the stimulants to passion which the modern towns afford.

The industry of these patient villagers is proverbial. They have a religious culture of their own, which often reaches remarkable heights of spiritual vision. There is also a depth of thought in their folk songs expressed in the simplest language. The poets of India usually come from these country homes. Great religious leaders have risen from them and left their names bright in the pages of Indian history.

Humble and lowly men and women with strikingly impressive personalities live ascetic lives in these villages seeking to find God. Their memory abides. The genius of India, in art, music, literature, architecture, has continually had its origin in them. Even among the most depressed classes saints have been born who have won the allegiance of posterity by their wisdom, piety, and devotion. They are still to be found to-day. In every part of India I have met them, and have felt the truth of the words of Christ: "I thank Thee, O Father, Lord of Heaven and Earth, because Thou hast hid these things from the worldly-wise and prudent, and hast revealed them unto babes. Even so, Father, for so it seemed good in Thy sight" (Matt. xi, 25).

Though these simple villagers may be babes in worldly wisdom, they are by no means lacking in strong moral sense and shrewd mother wit. As a whole they are intelligent, with a homely wisdom which comes chiefly from their constant touch with

Nature. Out of their rugged stock all that is best in India has been produced, from one generation to another, to the great enrichment of mankind. Their life is spent almost entirely out of doors, exposed to heat and cold, sun and rain, with only the barest covering of the body. An ethical code of domestic relationships has been worked out in a manner remarkably consonant with the village life itself. The community is like a larger family. Behind all there is a daily religious observance which has placed the greatest emphasis on self-control. It is true that these bounds are broken owing to the sexual urge in human nature, which is everywhere present. But the hard outward conditions do not continually provoke and stimulate passion until the whole character becomes vicious. While there is deplorable laxity on certain sides, there are also constant restraints.

Hindu religious custom is a very conservative medium acting on the inner life of each individual and going back countless generations in its origin and conception. It has become a part of the whole village system, exacting a discipline which is instinctively obeyed. Owing to its inhibitions with regard to eating, drinking, and marriage relations, the villagers become regulated in their habits. Some of their customs, which religion has sanctioned, are painfully oppressive, and these will come to our notice. But others have been found by long experience to have their great value as a discipline of the domestic life. While in some ways sex has been given scope, in others it has been subdued and restrained.

Hasty reform, therefore, even with regard to things which need to be changed or improved, is inadvisable. The new adjustment must be made with the greatest care, lest other evils are introduced and the last state is worse than the first.

After making very wide generalizations like these the real difficulty begins. For the differences in Indian village life, as I have witnessed them, are almost as marked as the underlying similarity of its texture.

In some parts, like Orissa, the whole country-side is stricken by constant malaria, flood, and famine, leaving a population sunk in want, addicted to opium, and therefore terribly depressed. On the other hand, in the Punjab and in Gujarat there is a peasantry, strong, virile, independent, retaining a simple hardihood of daily life untouched as yet by luxury or slothful ease. In the south of India, in spite of a tropical climate and a very meagre diet, there is an almost inexhaustible store of emotional energy, often, alas! running to waste. In Bengal artistic and literary genius, still to be found in the villages, is a marked feature. This has resulted in a wide literary renaissance in modern times. Sind and Rajputana are desert lands where mystical religious poetry has flourished age after age, uniting Hindu and Muslim saints in a common devotion. The Frontier Province has an independent and freedom-loving folk which follows Islam. Everywhere in the villages the absorption with religious songs and the recital of epics amounts almost to a passion.

The "plain living," of which Wordsworth speaks, is certainly to be found all over India. Is there also anything corresponding to what Wordsworth calls "high thinking"? The overwhelming load of indebtedness, which has been an alarming feature of this village life in modern times, has made such high thinking rarer, perhaps, to-day than before. Nevertheless, my own personal experience has been that in every part of India the problems of existence, the final mystery of God, the inner discipline of the soul, have a larger place in the thoughts of living men and women than anywhere else in the world. There is also a greater readiness on the part of some at least to abandon everything that man holds dear in search of the inner truth, when the voice within the soul commands. Religion still reigns supreme.

Such typical facts as these, that I have tried to describe, imply a deep restraining influence both of will and custom. The "plain living" is so severe that very few Europeans have been able to adapt themselves to its extreme simplicity. I have often been put to shame owing to the small requirements which I have still found necessary when I have lived in an Indian village, and also on account of the trouble I have given to these extremely poor but hospitable villagers merely to satisfy a few small personal needs. The one danger has been that they would go to some expense, which they could ill afford, in order to show their hospitality.

But beyond what I have described in this bare manner concerning a typical Indian village and its community life it is necessary at once to counterbalance the comparatively favourable judgment I have hitherto offered with the one adverse and demoralizing feature of untouchability. There are literally millions of the depressed classes who live on the outskirts of the villages in hovels of mud that are quite unfit for human habitation. They are usually in a state of indescribable misery and filth. Their faces reveal the semi-starvation that has reduced them to this sub-human existence. No language can be too strong to condemn the degradation that this pernicious system has brought to India. For it is unquestionably the greatest blot on Hindu society, and points to a deep-seated moral wrong whose curse will remain until the whole evil is finally abolished.

This subject will come before us at some length in another chapter; but it would have been unfair to write about Village India and to give no reference to it. So near the level of starvation are millions of these poor people that if it were not for the abundant sunshine, giving warmth and nourishment through the skin, it is doubtful whether it would be possible for a large portion of them to continue to exist at all. The words of Sir William Hunter, which refer chiefly to this class, have often been quoted, where he states that more than forty million people in India are living on only one meal a day or even less. They hardly know what it means to live without the pangs of hunger. What was true in his time, sixty years ago, is hardly less true to-day. Indeed, it is probable that the numbers he gives should be still further increased.

Those who know India best will agree that on the physical side this description which I have given only represents the bare truth, though exceptions may always be found in a whole sub-continent. They will also agree, if they have entered into the heart of the village life, that on the spiritual side I have not overdrawn the picture.

Yet facts like these appear to me convincingly to prove that the theory put forward with such assurance by these Western critics—that India's present misery is due to vicious habits of sexual excess—is profoundly wrong. It does not fit in with the facts. In the next chapter I shall continue this argument from a different standpoint.

Chapter 6

SOCIAL RESTRAINT

THE effect in Indian villages of this hard discipline may clearly be observed in the faces of the men and women. There is pain and hard endurance written across them in large characters; but very rarely is there that sensual look which would be almost universal if Miss Mayo's picture were correct.

I have wandered about all over India, often quite alone, from village to village, sharing the life and food of the people and wearing their dress. This has made me welcomed everywhere by the villagers as their friend. It is on the facts that I have gathered in this manner that I base my information. One thing more than any other has impressed me wherever I have gone, namely, the abstemious habits of the people. Nowhere in this world is life lived with such a complete absence of luxury of any kind among the masses of the population.

This habitual restraint may still further be observed from its slight reactions. Strangely enough, it seems to give way suddenly each year for a day or two especially at the time of the Holi Festival, in springtime, when licence often breaks through the dull surface of extreme monotony. But it is noticeable that immediately afterwards the even course of the daily life begins over again.

The one vast family extravagance is the marriage

festival. Then restrictions on expenditure entirely give way; and this event in a family will often lead to years of after-indebtedness. Yet psychologically, with such constant repression, this sudden outburst finds in a measure its own justification. I have seen the same thing happen in the poorest parts of England over "funerals" and other such events in the life of a poor family.

After the outline I have thus sketched it will easily be seen how untrue to fact the picture of Indian life must be which portrays it as almost wholly given over to sensuality and moral licence. The assertion, for instance, that seven or eight out of every ten young men between the ages of twenty-five and thirty become impotent owing to sexual excesses, is so palpably absurd when one reviews this village population that it hardly needs contradiction; and it is nothing short of a gross slander on India as a whole.

It is true that this declaration has been modified by the words "provided he has means to command his pleasure." But that proviso, in my opinion, only makes the phrase still more offensive. For I have lived in homes in different parts of India where ample means have existed for leading a sensual life of pleasure, but instead of this the pressure of moral self-restraint was so all-pervading as to be a perpetual wonder to me. A reference is made in Miss Mayo's book to the more healthy life of the country-side as obviating a part of the sexual excess imagined everywhere to prevail: and this reference shows that the facts I have tried so hard to make plain had actually come before her. But this abstemious and almost ascetic life of the country must, to an overwhelming degree, represent the normal state of India; for it cannot be repeated too often that the villages represent modern India rather than the towns. It follows, therefore, almost from her own admission, that the sexual life of India as a whole cannot possibly be so gross as she describes.

The town life, which has been precipitately pushed forward in Bombay and Calcutta and in a few other large cities, is in no sense typical of India in the same way and to the same degree that (for instance) the town element may be said to represent the English people. For the proportions are all reversed. In England the urban population far exceeds the rural; but in India the village people everywhere predominate. The towns are a growth of modern times, artificial and exotic. The villages have nestled amid their trees and along the river banks for centuries past. They are the true India.

The bulk of Hindu India, comprising the great majority of the Indian people (for three out of four are Hindus), maintains up to the present time in these numberless villages its own ultra-conservative customs. These are in need of reconstruction in very important respects, some of which will be dealt with later. But the main point which I desire to lay stress on is this. The whole of this intricate and closely woven domestic system stretching from one end of India to the other is remarkably free from purely evil obsessions of sex. I have watched Hindu women making their offerings at the wayside shrines, or near the river bathing ghats, whose faces were like that of a Madonna. It would be impossible to associate obscenity with such faces as these.

It is true, on the other hand, that there was an age of very gross coarseness in the past, coinciding with the massive temple architecture of the south: some of the carvings of certain Hindu temples are a disgrace for which no excuse should be offered. They should not thus be publicly exposed age after age with their moral filth. These, and the equally filthy stories of the gods and goddesses contained in certain Puranas, ought long ago to have been expunged. They can only do infinite harm. No defence should ever be made of them, for they are a sign of a diseased imagination and not of health.

The *devadasis*,[1] again, are one of those relics of that evil past; and their retention to-day, in connexion with some notorious temples, shows that the same passions still exist and are still shamefully encouraged. These poor girls have come to me, as their brother and friend, and implored me to help them. The elder ones among them have besought me to deliver their little daughters from their own inexpressibly miserable fate. I have sat with them hour after hour while they have mentioned, with bowed heads, their shame and wretchedness. All this I have told openly in the public Press, making no reservation; and my words, written from a tor-

[1] A *devadasi* is a temple woman who serves the vices of men.

tured heart, have never received a single word of condemnation from any Hindu, but only strong approval. Though myself a Christian and not a Hindu, I have been again and again asked to preside when this subject was being discussed in open conference; and my fellowship has been earnestly sought in helping to bring this gross evil, which is actually encouraged by debased religion, to an end.

Mahatma Gandhi has naturally been able to go much further than I have ever done. He has refused time after time, as a Hindu, to step inside these notorious temples. He has called them temples of Satan. He has declared that God is not to be found in them while they allow such evil deeds to be committed under the cloak of religion. This he has continually done with the strongest approval of all right-minded men and with very little open protest from reactionaries.

Undoubtedly, there are evil things like these in Hinduism to-day that deeply pain every well-wisher. They need to be exposed. Yet in order to get a *true* picture we must turn also to the deeper bedrock facts which are practically undisputed. The facts are these: that whatever excrescences have intervened to sap its vitality, whatever evil customs and traditions have spread like a creeper over it, the tree of Indian life is still sound at the centre. It is not rotten and decayed.

By nature I am, perhaps, fastidiously sensitive in these matters. The repulsion would be immediate if there were a coarse sensual background, festering all the while within those villages where I have lived and moved. As a matter of fact, any such sensitive repulsion in the presence of what is morally base has rarely happened to me while living in the midst of this simple country life in India close to the village people. There has been extraordinarily little among them, either in word or deed, that could be called gross or indecent.

All this has appeared to me to be due, not to the repression of sex, but rather to its lack of prominence as an all-engrossing theme. Where, however, I have been horribly repelled by something coarse and evil and sensual has been nearly always in the towns, or at some much-frequented pilgrim centre, such as Benares or Hardwar. There, in the faces of those who are pretending to carry out the *Sadhu* life, and also among those Pandas (as they are called) who make their living from the temples, I have been nauseated by a coarseness that filled me with utter disgust. Here there is a spiritual evil of the very worst type which can be felt in its defilement. No one would dream of defending it; nor could anyone fail to recognize the disgracefully low moral standards that accompany it. But this stands out in contrast to the village life itself and the simple religious observances of poor people. Long ago, when I lived in Delhi, it used to be one of my greatest pleasures to go out in the very early morning, just as the sun was rising, to the Kudsia Garden, where there was a pathway leading down to the River Jumna. At the ghat there was a shrine; and a long procession of Hindu women could always be seen going and returning along that pathway through the garden, bearing each of them a tray with offerings for worship at the shrine, especially the marigold, the favourite among the flowers. Many of these women would be up long before dawn, attending to some household duties before they went on their daily pilgrimage to the shrine. As they went and came back they would be singing their songs in chorus.

Such sights as these are common all over India wherever Hindu women worship. The sunlight would touch their white and coloured *saris* with the first rays of the sun, and as they passed me I could look into their faces and witness their devotion. How could one associate such scenes as these with pictures of utter moral decadence which Miss Mayo and others have drawn?

For hundreds of years, going back long before the birth of Christ, this immemorial custom of the East, to go out to the river bank in order to worship at the break of dawn, has been observed with unbroken succession in each generation. Customs such as these do not imply sexual decadence. The Hindu religion which encourages them has its strong ascetic side.

Of one thing I would bear special witness; and the emphasis that I would lay upon it is paramount in this connexion. The natural modesty and simplicity of the Indian women have impressed me more and more deeply every year that I have lived among them. After long journeys all over the world I have come back to this with renewed thankfulness as one of the most beautiful things in human life. As a man of religion, trusted and respected, I have met those who live in seclusion as well as those who are not bound by any such strict customs.

The ordinary word by which every Indian woman is addressed is either "sister" or "mother," according to the age of the person. The habit of using these words is not confined to those who are near relations in one family, or even to close neighbours. They are applied to people who are met as visitors or strangers. Servants use them towards those who are set over them in the household. They are not empty or formal symbols, but contain a world of meaning. The gentle quality of Indian womanhood corresponds to them. For it is the sisterly and motherly element that always predominates in domestic duties and in friendly greetings.

There is an historical fact which has always appeared to me to be singularly convincing as final evidence. The civilization of India, which goes back so far in the past, is still young. With amazing rapidity it is transforming itself to-day and casting aside age-long abuses. Such a perpetual spring of energy could never be put forth by a decadent, sex-ridden people.

Therefore, instead of the sex passion being "the one subject of conversation," instead of songs dealing with it being "eternally on the lips of Indian women," as these books suggest, the motherly and sisterly relations are those that come to the front in human intercourse. They are the qualities that I have learnt to look upon as most typical of Indian rural life.

Chapter 7

THE JOINT FAMILY

HITHERTO in this book I have dealt chiefly with the gross misrepresentations concerning the state of Indian society that have been widely published in the West. In doing so I have pointed out that in no country in the whole world to-day are reforms of old abuses being so rapidly and thoroughly carried out. I have also given what seems to me an adequate answer to the accusation that abnormal sexual indulgence has been the ruin of India and the cause of all her poverty.

It will now be necessary to explain in outline some of the chief differences in the domestic life of the East that mark it off from the type we are familiar with in Europe. For in dealing with a civilization like that of India we have to be very careful not to condemn that which has stood the test of centuries merely because it is unlike anything that we ourselves have experienced.

There are two special features in Indian society which need careful and sympathetic study if we are to understand India at all. The former of these is the joint family system, and the second is caste. In both instances it will be best first of all to trace their history, and then afterwards to assess their place in this modern world wherein we live to-day.

The joint family, which is one of the main

features of Indian social life, dates back to the earliest period of civilization in the East. It has impressed its mark on Hinduism most of all, but has also profoundly influenced the other religions which have found their home in India. Its roots lie very deep in the Indian soil, and it is doubtful if the modern idea of domestic life, as it has developed in the West, will ever be able either to uproot it or supplant it.

What is meant by a joint family is this: that brothers as they grow up to manhood, instead of living separately in separate houses, combine together and occupy the different rooms of a single house along with their children and their children's children. The daughters of the family, on becoming married, leave the father's house and become members of the joint family to which their husbands belong. Thus the sons of the family bring the daughters of other families into the household of which they themselves are members. The head of the family is the eldest among the brothers.

The mother has always her own place of honour as well as the father, and her status in the home is in certain respects supreme. In purely domestic matters she rules and guides. The tie between the mother and her sons is very close indeed. They are her jewels. The son's reverence for his mother in India is beyond all expression in words. In innumerable instances it is the deepest thing in his life and shapes his life's course. The loss of his mother is the heaviest blow that can happen to a son.

The number of those who thus live together under one roof may be very large indeed. Reckoning in the grandchildren and even the great-grandchildren (for marriage is early in India, and generations follow one another in quick succession), it may number over a hundred members. The household servants, who have often grown up with the family, have their recognized place. They become deeply attached to the family tradition. They often call the individual members by familiar names without any disrespect. In some ways I have been reminded of the clan relationships in the North of Scotland, but it is difficult in modern times to get any close analogy in the West.

On very many occasions I have been admitted into such a family as I have here described, both as a friend and a guest, and have therefore been able to see something of its inner significance. It is a mode of living which obviously calls for the play of kindly affection and good humour on a larger scale than domestic life in Europe. For in the West the newly wedded couple leave the father's home and "set up house" together for themselves alone. Here it is clear that a different form prevails from that which is known in the East.

The development of this Eastern system came about through simple and natural causes. The abundance of fertile soil in the vast alluvial plains of India and China, at a time when population was scanty and labour was precarious, lent itself to a large family unit wherein all its kindred members who were able to work remained together and laboured together. This formed an early experiment in co-partnership on the basis of kinship. When it proved successful it became an integral part of the ancient rural economy; for it kept the land as it received cultivation in the hands of the family, and the ancestral home was occupied by each generation in turn.

But beyond all this there was a strong religious bond in the worship of the *pitris*, or ancestors. The performance of this worship was a primary religious duty which held the family together by sacred ties not lightly broken. Thus religion added its sanction to that which had already proved by experiment its own economic worth.

Some of the advantages of the joint family system have been lucidly explained by one who has recently died, but left behind him an invaluable book, published after his death by his widow as a sacred duty. Dr. Kunhikannan of Mysore writes as follows:—

"The association in one household of married couples, parents, and grandparents tends to soften the angularities of temperament and habit. Of collisions of temper and habit, jealousies and suspicions, there ought to be no occasion in the household. The elder members will moderate the impetuosity of the younger, and the patience and experience and the wider perspectives of the elder would limit the youthful enthusiasms and indiscretions of the younger and prevent much of their cruder manifestations. There is restraint right through the household, the restraint from word or deed that might cause offence or pain. There is respect for the elders, tenderness for the sick and maimed. Within there is one wonderful spirit of equality which demands equal share in income, as well as in feasts and festivities, irrespective of age and infirmity. . . . What is good for one is good for all. No special favour is allowed to be shown by any mother to her children which may not be shared by other children in the household. . . .

"The joint family affords the best training in the humanities. Love and affection carried beyond the narrow circle of the family to embrace relations of the second and third degree, and the close adjustment necessary in a family of many members living together, all based on an intimate knowledge of their qualities and feelings, help to develop the understanding and cultivate the emotions."

One very remarkable result has followed from this larger family system. There has never been, as far as I am aware, in India, the need of a poorhouse or workhouse, run by the State, to which paupers go as a last refuge. For there will always be *some* place in the family where at least the daily bread may be obtained; and up to the present that last desperate state of misery, where not even a single relative is left to give shelter, is mercifully absent from India, with its family bonds stretching out so far and wide. Whether there may not now be the need of such a refuge, since the family bonds have become weakened by the advance of modern civilization, remains yet to be seen.

What has always seemed a strange thing to me, in my ignorance of what an upbringing means in such a joint family, is that there have not been more pioneers in the past who have gone far and wide abroad seeking adventure, while those dependent on them remained behind, well looked after under the paternal care of the head of the family. For anxiety concerning wife and children must be immensely lessened when they are left in such safe keeping. It may be the case that the adventurous side of human character is softened by the continued give-and-take which the joint family system requires. The individual initiative becomes weakened at the very time that the gentler side of life is strengthened. Dr. Kunhikannan would admit this limitation, but suggests at the same time that there is more staying power—more of the qualities described in the Tao Teh King of Lao-tze, which in a singular manner both China and India appear to have made their own. There is less, he would say, of the strong aggressive and acquisitive character of the West. He writes:—

"What individualistic societies have, in the greater play of Self, is but a temporary advantage. It is by no means certain that they will or can maintain the individual will at its present sharpness and vigour. One has only to watch the progress of new movements, and the course of their history, to realize that there is a new orientation of Western society, in which the free play of the individual will becomes more and more limited, and may become subject to conditions similar or analogous to those that have developed under the joint family."

There is something remarkably akin in this philosophy to that of China, where the Tao bids us:—

"Temper your sharpness, disentangle your ideas, moderate your brilliance, and live in harmony with your age."

In another place we read:—

"I have three precious things which I hold fast and prize—gentleness, frugality, and humility."

In another chapter, where Indian character is frankly discussed, I have pointed out how the very weakness of subjection under a foreign yoke was made still more pronounced owing to an almost complete absorption in the interests of the family group which it engendered—a kind of *family* selfishness, whereby the safety of the family was placed before any other earthly ambition; wherein the foreign rule drove the character of the individual more and more to take refuge within the home and to neglect the larger interests of the nation and also of humanity itself. This is a danger which Dr. Kunhikannan himself would recognize. Yet I would not end my criticism on that note, but rather would refer once again to the very remarkable qualities which the joint family system is able to foster—its wide tolerances, its humanism, its tranquillity of spirit in a world of feverish haste and bigotry and strife.

If the prayer which Christ taught the West is truly the prayer of the family—Our Father—then we who have learnt from infancy to pray this prayer ought to be humble enough to receive some of the great lessons of this larger family life, where the East has gone far beyond us in exploring the home virtues to which men and women may aspire. We should also note that in these two countries, India and China, where the joint family system has been most cultivated, the spirit of peace has flourished most. Even in this modern age it still remains deeply rooted in the human heart. If then we seek to abolish war, may not the East have here something to teach us which is of profound importance?

It may be that the East, on the other hand, has something to learn from the West, and that the ancient word of the Jewish Scripture, "For this cause shall a man leave father and mother and cleave unto his wife: and they twain shall be one flesh," has a message for India and China, giving an individuality and a nobility to woman which is difficult to attain under the joint family system with its patriarchal basis. However that may be, there is surely far too much to learn from one another to allow time for disputing in harsh and contemptuous terms about differences. One of the reasons I have chosen to quote so largely from Dr. Kunhikannan in this chapter is because the note of bitterness is absent from his writing. His desire to be fair to the Western system is transparent.

I have already mentioned the possibility that the larger family life of India and China may have qualities that might prove to be an antidote for that war mentality which has now obsessed the West. There is one further neurosis from which the West is suffering that may also find healing power by a closer attention to the East. The family unit to-day in Europe and America is becoming smaller and smaller. A household with no children at all, or with only one child, is by no means uncommon. How are these isolated children to grow up with all the daily smoothing away of angularities which education in a large family imperceptibly produces? How can the *virtues* of a large family be revived?

When I was a boy it was my good fortune to be one of a family of fourteen children, out of whom thirteen grew to a full age, and the discipline of give-and-take which this meant for me every day of my life was an untold blessing. We were a marvellously happy and united family, and have remained so ever since. It is true that the days of such large families are now past in the West, but among those who pray the Lord's Prayer—the prayer of the family—may there not be a renewed effort made for a joint family life? This might not be an exact copy of the East, but it might nevertheless contain some of its virtues.

So close are these family ties in the East that cousins living in the same house are treated as brothers and called by the name of brothers. If a father dies, his own brother as a matter of course takes the whole responsibility of the education and maintenance of the children, just as if his brother's children were his own. I have seen noble things of this kind happening in India among my own students even in the midst of their college course, and have been deeply touched by the way they will undertake a heavy burden of responsibility without a single murmur or even a thought of self. All this has shown me possibilities of this larger family affection that I had never realized in so full a measure until I came to the East.

Yet one further question. May not a community life be possible in the West, comprising many families wherein the *spiritual* relationship becomes so close that such things as those that happen daily in India are made possible on a higher plane?

Bishop Westcott of Durham, while he was Canon of Peterborough, wrote much about a joint family system of this character. He also sought earnestly to make a practical experiment in which his own family would join. Modern psychology has taught us, after thorough research on the subject, that the group wherein human life is lived to the best advantage must be neither too small nor too large. The solitary child, living alone with its parents, is an example of the former. The barrack-like boarding school, where boys are herded together, is an example of the latter. What I have often observed in India, while living as a guest in a joint family, has seemed to me again and again to hit the happy mean. On that account it has appeared to be worthy of special study by those who are painfully seeking to find out the weaknesses and flaws in our modern civilization in the West.

Chapter 8

CASTE IN INDIA

THE subject of caste is one of the least understood in the West, and much ignorant criticism has been written about it. Even among Indians themselves different explanations have been given which have tended only to obscure its meaning. Yet just as the joint family system and the village community are both typically characteristic of India from earliest times, so caste has been a part of Indian civilization for more than three thousand years. It is obvious, therefore, that it must originally have served some useful purpose which brought benefit to the community as a whole; otherwise it would never have possessed such a remarkable survival value.

Before condemning caste, root and branch, to-day on account of some retrograde features which have become connected with it, the better course would be to study its origins and to diagnose what historically lies hidden beneath its outer surface. We can then ascertain whether such recognized evils as "child marriage" and "untouchability" are inherent in the system or are excrescences which need to be removed.

Such an analysis is all the more necessary because the caste system, as generally explained, gives such a shock to a liberal and democratic European that he is hardly prepared even to discuss the question seriously, and only wonders why an anachronism of this kind is allowed to go on surviving and cumbering the ground so long.

Yet no one who has travelled widely in other parts of the world can have failed to recognize that caste exists to-day in certain foreign countries, and that a new caste system has begun to take shape wherever a superior civilization impinges on one that is inferior. Both in South Africa and in the south of the United States of America this is a burning question. History has repeated itself. There is no problem more acute in these new countries than this caste or "colour" question.

Let us see first what happened in India more than three thousand years ago. The fair-skinned Aryan invaders from the north were suddenly brought into contact with the original inhabitants of the country, who were of a different colour and culture from themselves. The Aryan took steps to segregate himself and refused to mingle his blood. He made a sharp division between himself and the darker race, and thus established "caste." In the same manner the Boer in South Africa, as he went up from the Cape to the Transvaal, was brought into hostile contact with the dark-skinned Bantu warriors. When the land was settled at last these Bantus were forced to become the serfs of the Boer farmers, and they have remained much in the same position ever since. The Grondwet, or fundamental law of the Transvaal, was thus written: "There shall be no equality between white and black either in Church or State." Just as in ancient India, so among the Boers, religion was brought in to make this racial segregation secure.

In the United States the southern sugar and cotton belt was cultivated by slaves introduced from West Africa. These were settled in slavery among the fair-skinned colonials from Europe. Here again the same problem arose of two races, at two different stages of culture, living side by side in the same area. During the period of slavery itself the segregation was one of status. There were "slaves" and "masters." But even after the emancipation the colour bar has remained fixed.

The problem in all these cases was as follows:—Should intermarriage be freely allowed between the two races, or should the strongest possible sanctions be fixed against it? Should social intermingling and the sharing of common food at the same table be allowed, or should it be forbidden?

In ancient India—as also in these two modern instances—the average man decided vehemently and even violently against any intermixture whatever taking place. Hence the beginning of what in India was developed into the caste system. The dark inhabitants after conquest were allotted the status of *Sudras* by the invaders. The word implied any lower kind of service, and originally marked inferiority of status. There were no wars of extermination, although there was much fierce and savage fighting. In the long run the colour bar was strictly imposed. The Aryans were called the "twice born." They were allowed to wear the sacred thread and hear the sacred scriptures read aloud. The Sudras were not allowed to do either. They were kept in perpetual subordination.

That this was the origin of caste is in my opinion certain. The original Sanskrit word *varna* means "colour"; and however learned scholars may dispute about it, those of us who have seen those parts of the world where the same problem is acute can have no doubt at all in our own minds that what we see happening to-day gives the correct interpretation of the ancient Indian system. But considerable uncertainty remains about the division of the Aryan invaders themselves into the three higher, or "twice born," castes of Brahmins, Kshatriyas, and Vaishyas. Some have postulated three different invasions, the earlier of which mingled their blood with the dark original inhabitants. But there seems to be no need for such an hypothesis and there are no clear historical records.

The simplest solution of the problem appears to be that "occupation" took the place of "race" and "colour" in making this minor division. The sharp dividing line remained fixed between the "twice born" and the Sudras. Further divisions among the "twice born" themselves carried no stigma with them. They were rather class distinctions.

Thus between the higher castes we find at first no such hard and fast rules against intermarriage as existed with regard to the Sudras. The Brahmin remained steadfast in his ritual and priestly functions. The Kshatriya became the warrior and ruler: the Vaishya became the landlord and merchant. The Sudra, in those early days, was more or less like a serf attached to the soil. With him alone at first marriage was completely banned.

So far we have been covering historical ground, and the conclusions we have reached may be regarded as fairly accurate. How "untouchability" arose is somewhat more difficult to trace. Probably certain of the aboriginals, because of their unclean habits of eating carrion, became regarded as polluted. Then others, who were outcasted because of some marriage irregularity or some grave moral offence, were placed in the same class as "untouchable." These were reckoned in rank below the Sudras and called Namasudras. Another name, Panchama, means literally the "Fifth Caste," i.e. below the four main castes.

We shall come across the evil effects of this "outcasting" in a later chapter. In what follows, by way of historical analysis, it is only necessary to attempt to explain the development of the whole system during different periods of Indian history.

In the fifth century B.C. the full floodtide of Buddhism began to sweep over India. While it left alone for the most part the old religious Hindu ritual, its fundamental principles involved a casteless society. The story of the monk Ananda receiving water at the hands of an outcaste woman implies this. But the evil of untouchability had already become very deep-seated, and when the Brahmin supremacy revived, after a thousand years of Buddism, the lines of demarcation between one caste and another were made stronger instead of weaker. The whole caste system became stratified, and innumerable divisions into sub-castes began also to be formed.

When the Muhammadan invasions began in A.D. 1000, and were repeated year after year, Hindu society, already divided into castes, had no corporate unity wherewith to resist them. Magnificent bravery was shown by some of the warrior castes, but society itself was hopelessly divided. The evil lot of the Sudras and outcastes made them indifferent as to whether their rulers were Muslims or Hindus. In the course of centuries immense numbers went over to Islam, which has now reached eighty million souls, most of whom have been drawn from the lower castes in the villages of north and east India. In Bengal the exodus from Hinduism was greatest. In the Punjab also the Muslim population was largely increased both by conversion and invasion.

Orthodox Hindu religion retired more and more into its own impenetrable fortress. Only among the Hindu Bhakti Saints[1] was there an attempt made to break down the barriers of caste and meet Islam itself on the highest platform of worship offered to the one Supreme God. Ramananda, Kabir, Chaitanya, Dadu, Nanak—all show the true spirit of love and unity which sought to do away with these inhuman class distinctions. There is no nobler period in Hindu religious history than this.

[1] Those who preached devotion to God as personal and loving mankind.

But side by side with these great reformers a hardening was taking place in the priestly ranks all along the line. A passive resistance struggle began against any further encroachments of Islam, and this sowed the seeds of deep bitterness for the future. Those who had carried forward the teaching of the Bhakti saints were compelled to start new sects. The most remarkable of these is the Sikh community, wherein no caste is observed and no child marriage takes place. It owes its origin to Guru Nanak and its final form to Guru Govind. The Kabir Panthis and the Dadu Panthis also retain in some measure the teaching of Kabir and Dadu.

Thus, on the one hand, in the north of India the ties of caste were being loosened and the "untouchables" were being more humanely treated. But on the other hand, at the ancient religious centres where the Brahmin priesthood was strong, these caste restrictions, owing to the doctrine of caste pollution, were drawn tighter than ever.

In the south of India this Brahmin ascendancy assumed an even more unbending character, and as a consequence rules about pollution and segregation became indefinitely extended. The treatment of the pariah or outcaste was more and more inhuman, as will be described later. At the same time it is a happiness to relate that the revolt against the whole evil system of "caste pollution" has found its noblest champions among the Brahmins themselves.

In the United Provinces, with their ancient pilgrim shrines at Benares, Allahabad, Muttra,

Brindaban, and Hardwar, the conservative forms of Hinduism largely prevail. The evils connected with the caste system have not been abolished. Western India has suffered from a rigid form of "untouchability" in the past, but owing to Mahatma Gandhi and his wife Kasturbai a rapid change for the better is being accomplished. In Bengal and the Punjab, partly owing to the large numbers of Muslims among the village population and partly to the reforming movements, the grip of "untouchability" has been loosened.

To-day in India the whole caste system is passing through the fire of the furnace, which will test it and purge it seven times over. It may be that it will be unable to stand the test. Some of India's greatest religious leaders and thinkers, such as Rabindranath Tagore, have almost given up hope of reformation from within now being possible. Yet he would be the first to demand that the useful purposes of racial adjustment which caste once fulfilled—however crudely—should not be undone. Other means should be adopted for bringing the different communities in India together on a far wider basis than the present stratification of caste.

While writing this chapter on a very difficult subject, I have endeavoured to remain throughout as objective as possible, putting down the simplest historical facts. In other sections of this book the relation of the caste system to such evils as child marriage and untouchability will be dealt with in much fuller detail; but it was necessary first of all to explain something of the origin of caste itself. For nothing can be more important for anyone who has never been to India, and yet wishes to gain an intelligent view of the Hindu social system, than to get ideas straight about caste. There are few things harder to understand, and yet more necessary to appreciate rightly. If, therefore, a friendly understanding is to be reached at all, this whole issue cannot be neglected.

Those of us who feel most deeply the need of friendship between the two countries have to leave aside altogether the superior attitude where Indian customs differ from our own, and make an honest effort instead to find out as nearly as possible where the difference lies.

Chapter 9

MARRIAGE AND CASTE

WOMANHOOD, in a climate like India, begins at least three years earlier than in a cold climate such as England. To show how vast the difference is, I would quote the following passage from a book entitled *Kenya from Within*.[1] The writer states: "For English children, Kenya is a forcing house. Girls of ten and eleven may be found who are as developed physically as girls of sixteen in Britain—miniature women in fact."

This modifies the whole aspect of marriage in the tropics. The late marriages in England and America are obviously unsuitable to the East. Indeed, most thoughtful men believe that marriages have been delayed too long in the West.

What has to be realized on both sides is this: that mistakes have been made by East and West alike which will have to be rectified in time. The stress of one peculiar set of circumstances has forced back the age of marriage too early in the East. The stress of another set of circumstances has forced forward the age of marriage too late in the West.

Both sides have gone to the extreme point. Thus marriages delayed till the age of thirty or even later for women, such as now not unfrequently happen

[1] *Kenya from Within*. W. MacGregor Ross. Published by George Allen & Unwin Ltd.

in Western countries owing chiefly to economic causes, are surely unnatural. The large number of spinsters who never marry at all, because no opportunity is given them, cannot represent a healthy social condition. On the Eastern side child marriages, between the ages of twelve and fourteen, are surely against nature. The large number of Indian widows, including child-widows, who may never marry again, has also its own adverse effect on society. When both sides are thus in the wrong, the worst thing of all is to start a campaign of mutual recrimination.

The time is now ripe for reform both in the East and the West, and it will gradually be carried out. What is needed is intelligent sympathy with the difficulties that have to be met on both sides, not ignorant abuse. It would have been quite easy for Indian writers to publish accounts taken from unimpeachable Western sources setting forth the moral chaos, owing to frequent divorce, that now exists in the West. But hitherto they have been on the whole too courteous and considerate to employ such "poison gas" methods of controversy.

A second point, which is liable to be greatly misunderstood in the West, is the question of a second marriage in India while the first wife is still living. In many indirect ways the impression has been received abroad that polygamy is a frequent factor in India. Because certain rajas and maharajas have been lax in their marriage affairs and have married more than one wife in order to increase their progeny, or indulge in a life of pleasure, it has been wrongly assumed that polygamy is very widely practised. Ideas in the West on this subject are often ludicrously incorrect. This does not mean, of course, that polygamy should be condoned or excused where a high civilization is aimed at: but the facts about its practice in India have been distorted.

When I was in South Africa recently I had often to dispel erroneous ideas on this subject; and I found it very difficult to do so owing to ignorant pre-conceptions. So I took the census figures, which showed that over 98 per cent of Indian marriages, including both Hindu and Muslim, are monogamous to-day. It may be regarded as certain that even this very slight proportion of polygamous marriages will still further diminish as education advances.

There is, however, sadly enough, but little public condemnation of a polygamous marriage where some great maharaja is concerned. But that is due to the glamour of royalty which still holds the popular mind. It does not go deeper or further.

Looking back over the whole of the time I have lived in India, I cannot personally remember having made the acquaintance of any Indian who was married to two wives at the same time. Thus it is entirely wrong to regard India, as a whole, as a polygamous country. Indeed, if power were entirely in Indian hands, it might not be found difficult within a short period to make monogamy the law of the land, as Mustafa Kemal has done in Turkey.

With regard to the present polygamous marriages of Indian rajas and maharajas, which I have referred to above as an exception, we have only to remember the past history of morganatic marriages within the royal families of Europe to see that India is not alone in this laxity towards royalty. We have to be patient, till the mass mind is ready to treat kings and queens as ordinary human beings.

Divorce is never practised in Hinduism. Up to the present the very idea of divorce is repellent to those Hindus who have deep religious feeling. There is no laxity whatever here; indeed, the trend of future social legislation will probably be in the direction of releasing from a life bondage those whose marriages have been a deadly failure and can hardly be called marriages at all. Islam retains the right of divorce; but it is interesting to note how seldom divorce happens in Muslim India compared with other lands. The Hindu tradition remains very strong, even among those who for generations past have embraced Islam. The same may be said with regard to Indian Christians. Divorce among them also is exceedingly rare.

One of the normal customs peculiar to orthodox Hindu India, as life is lived to-day, is that no widow should be remarried. It has been made abundantly clear, from the times of Vidyasagar, that this represents no integral part of original Hindu religion. It is rather a custom that has gained the sanction of religion, and it has led to innumerable evils of a very grave and often intolerable character. For the custom has made even the betrothal ceremony (which may take place in early childhood) just as sacred in this respect as marriage itself. Girls who have been betrothed but not actually married are, in orthodox Hindu families, not allowed to marry again, even if the boy to whom the girl is betrothed dies when both are quite young. The young girl is regarded as a widow all the same. This means that these young girls, who when they grew up might have been happy mothers with families of their own, are condemned to a perpetual "widowhood" without ever having known a husband or lived even for a few months a normal married life. The great leaders of India to-day have condemned this cruel practice. The force of public opinion is turning against it, especially in the north; and every reform movement within Hinduism has set its face towards its removal.

The acute misery that often accompanies this enforced widowhood is a blot on the Hindu social system. It is true that the number of marriages among such child-widows is increasing. Mahatma Gandhi and Rabindranath Tagore have been among the strongest advocates of such marriages. Tagore has given his son in marriage to a young widow. But progress is still very slow, because India is a conservative country and the villages are scattered. In the south the rate of advance is much slower than in the north.

The actual treatment of the Hindu widow varies greatly, even between one family and another, and also within local areas. At least that has been my own experience. In many instances I have found their fate to be a miserably sad one, and the common idea of a widow's lot is that of misery and sorrow.

There is something utterly incongruous to the modern mind in the widower being rapidly hurried by his relations into a second marriage, even with one who may be twenty years younger than himself, with no observance of fasts or disciplines for his dead wife, while the widow undergoes all these hardships and is never allowed to remarry. This cruel inequality of sex relations must surely be abolished as soon as woman takes her true place in society.

I am fully aware that the modern mind itself is not infallible in these matters, and that the whole question of the relation of the family to society cannot be settled in a day—especially in such Eastern countries as India and China, where the social genius of the people has insisted on the family, rather than the individual, being regarded as the unit. We have to respect that point of view, and to consider carefully its whole moral bearing, before we seek to criticize its details. We have also to come to a much clearer understanding about the changes which the modern humanitarian mind really requires. We must not make the last state of things worse than the first, and thus add to the chain of human ill.

But what can be truly said is this. The men of India have now at last fully recognized the burden which, by a cruel destiny, the widow has had to bear in the supposed interests of society. They have also learnt to regard widows, who have come up to their ideal of self-sacrifice for the good of the social order, with a true and deep reverence of spirit. On the whole, this is the aspect of widowhood in India that has specially attracted my attention and won my regard. When it became embodied during mediaeval times in an act like *Sati*, its extravagance became obvious; and when Raja Ram Mohan Roy, more than a century ago, worked along with Lord Bentinck for its removal, the conscience of social India passively accepted the change, though the ideas connected with *Sati* still lingered. There was no popular revolt against this drastic alteration of the Hindu social system when it was passed into law.

But the ideal of the true *Sati*—that is to say, the wife who prefers to die with her husband—still remains very strong indeed. One of the pictures of modern India that has touched the heart is that called *Sati*, by Nandalal Bose. It interested me to find how the late Principal Rudra of Delhi, the son of an Indian Christian and himself utterly devoted to the Christian ideal, explained to me shortly before his death that nothing could shake from his mind this ideal of a Hindu wife which had become embodied in legend and song. He regarded it as one of the most sacred things in the whole world. His words made a profound impression on me uttered at such a time and by such a noble spirit. They checked some of the hasty conclusions which I had previously drawn. For my own mind had swung very far the other way.

Let me add, from my own experience, that there is often a respect for the widow in a large number of Hindu families that is altogether gracious. She wins the reverence of the household by her goodness, piety, and self-denial. She becomes the bearer of all burdens. Very often, like charity, she suffers long and is kind. The little children especially soon learn to love one who is so gentle to them on all occasions, and she finds her home in their hearts. All this inner side of Indian domestic life I have seen at close quarters, and it has won my deep regard and has explained to me what Principal Rudra told me. But it needs to be repeated at the same time with equal emphasis that there are other Hindu widows who are treated by the whole household in a very different manner, so that their lives become joyless and loveless. Among these Hindu widows the suffering is unending, and all Indian social reformers are anxious to remove their misery. The cruellest thing of all is when superstition casts in the young widow's face the rebuke that *she* has brought ill-luck to the house. Under that hideous idea lurk often untold hardships and humiliations.

A third fact which ought to be carefully remembered in the West is this: that the peculiar social system underlying the whole structure of Hindu religion, called caste, had once served (as I have already tried to show) a useful purpose.[1] It safeguarded marriage, encouraged an abstemious domestic life, and gave to Indian homes a stern discipline

[1] See Chapter 8, pp. 92, 95 and 96.

at a time when it was most needed. Caste is antiquated to-day in its present form, and sorely requires reconstruction on modern lines of absolute equality between man and man and also between man and woman. But formerly it helped to establish the supreme sanctity of the home and curb the unruly passions of mankind. In so far as the virtues of a peaceful and temperate character have become embodied in Hindu society, this is due in a very large measure to that ancient organic structure of caste which Hinduism had originated. For the domestic principles underlying married life were strictly regulated by the different caste rules and observances. In this way the common tenets of Hinduism, inculcating the sanctity of marriage, were brought home to the simple village people. The gravest fault in the whole system was the almost complete subordination and even subjection of the wife to the husband. This goes back to the laws of Manu, and has depressed womanhood in India more than anything else.

After many years I have come to know, at first hand, the deep penetration which the Hindu religion has made into every part of the social and domestic fabric. It has become the warp and woof of the texture of Indian village life. This texture is still, for the most part, unimpaired by the ravages of time. It holds fast in some of the most critical relations of life. Yet in other respects it is antiquated and outworn beyond any repair.

If those who write so disparagingly about India

had seen the results that have occurred when the wholesome marriage influences under the Hindu system had suddenly been destroyed, with nothing to put in their place, they would have realized how carefully directed the new reformation in India must be, if the present evils of caste are to be eliminated and its good features preserved.

For on the one hand I have witnessed in the British colonies the terrible demoralization wrought by an evil form of labour called the "indenture system," wherein the family life was broken up and men and women were herded together. On the other hand, I have seen with immense relief and happiness, when indenture was abolished, how the old customary moral order became restored and a wholesome family life built up again, simply owing to the deep-rooted tradition of Hindu marriage which had held its ground among these agricultural village folk. As soon as ever they were free from indenture they began to reconstruct their social and domestic life on customary Hindu lines. At the same time they were able to leave behind many of the evil things which in India had been intermingled with the good.

No one would be less willing or ready than I to defend these ancient evils which have grown up within the caste system. But there is the spirit of the iconoclast, which in India must always be avoided. Many people, including some who are ardent missionaries, have written about the glaring evils which have come later into Hindu life without considering the deep lesson taught in a parable by Christ Himself. For in the story of the wheat and the tares the warning is given by Him concerning premature interference. That parable is true for all time. Everything in modern anthropology is corroborating its wisdom, and Christian workers ought to be the first to study its inner meaning while retaining, along with it, their earnest zeal for reform.

The reason for this is that all true and lasting change must proceed from within. It cannot be effected from the outside. To take a simple but striking illustration from another field of work, new sanitary methods are invaluable for India in order to eliminate diseases like hook-worm, dysentery, and cholera. We have in our hands to-day immensely more powerful preventive weapons than we ever had before. There is immediate scope for work of this kind, and it is being bravely carried on by those who have been fully trained to undertake it. The Rockefeller Institute workers and many medical missionaries, as well as a whole host of Indian workers themselves who have been instructed in Western science, are earning the gratitude of the villagers of India by their patient laborious work. *But it is necessary always for such new knowledge and scientific method to be assimilated and appropriated by the village people themselves, if it is to have any lasting value.* It cannot be hurriedly dictated and imposed from outside. Above all, it must not create new fear and suspicion.

This implies that the official who comes from

abroad, and even the voluntary helper, such as the missionary, can do very little, unless the hearts of the people have been touched and the strangeness of the "foreigner" has entirely passed away and been forgotten. The final test must come from the people themselves.

Chapter 10

CHILD MARRIAGE

On no single point does Miss Mayo lay more stress throughout the whole of her book than on the deterioration of Indian life owing to the defects of child marriage. It may be taken as one of her main themes. Here, as elsewhere, her extreme exaggeration has spoilt the very object she wished to achieve.

"Take," she says, "a girl child of twelve years old, a pitiful physical specimen in bone and blood, illiterate, ignorant, without any sort of training in habits of health. Force motherhood upon her at the earliest possible moment. . . ."

"The Indian girl," she continues, "in common practice, looks for motherhood nine months after reaching puberty, or anywhere between the ages of fourteen and eight. The latter age is extreme, although in some sections not exceptional: the former is well above the average."

She blames everyone in turn for not having had the common sense to deal with Indian miseries from this standpoint, and she assumes that her main statement will go altogether uncontradicted. She blames the social reformers for keeping silence, or else indulging in flattery, and declares that no one among them is sufficiently a true and sincere friend to hold up the mirror and show that it is *this* more than anything else which is sapping Indian vitality. Thus the general impression given to the average reader is that no one has really tackled this vast subject properly and dealt with it drastically enough until *she* came to India and exposed it.

It is strange indeed that in her book, and in literature of similar character, there is practically no recognition whatever of the devoted and unselfish service which has been given by men and women who have borne the burden and heat of the day and have worked in every part of India to bring about the very reforms which she advocates. One of the greatest of these has been the poet, Rabindranath Tagore, whom she condemns as a reactionary, so reckless has she been in her judgment of other people.

The truth is that the long succession of social and religious workers in the provinces, where child marriage had most prevailed, has made its deep impression. This is perhaps especially noticeable in recent years in Bengal; but Gujarat and other parts of India have shown similar progress. The Punjab has always kept the age of marriage higher than the other provinces. Within the important Sikh community, and also in the Arya Samaj, it has always been as high as the requirements of physical fitness demand.

Since the time when extreme statements were published by Miss Mayo a great deal has been written on this subject which may be briefly summarized here. From every side it has been authoritatively shown that her hasty generalizations were inaccurate. Her documentation itself was incorrect. A very large number of maternity cases have been quoted by different doctors, who had statistics at their disposal, which go to prove that this premature motherhood of which Miss Mayo speaks is now comparatively rare.

To take, for instance, the maternity cases in Madras Maternity Hospital—where 2,312 mothers were delivered of their *first* babies—86 per cent were seventeen years or over. Out of nearly 4,300 cases of first motherhood in other parts of India *only thirteen were below fifteen years of age*. Authorities having at their disposal the largest experience of Indian conditions have stated that these first child-birth records are a fair index of what is going on in most parts of the country, though in certain communities premature marriages still continue more frequently than these figures indicate.

One of the most striking figures of the census of 1921 (which was the census on which Miss Mayo relied for her statistics) is this: that at the age of fifteen more than 60 per cent of the girls of India remained unmarried. This one fact obviously renders untenable her main statement already quoted above, that "the Indian girl in common practice looks for motherhood nine months after reaching puberty, or anywhere between the ages of fourteen and eight."

In corroboration of these statistics of child-birth it also needs to be remembered that the marriage ceremony in India by no means implies immediate consummation. Sir Denzil Ibbetson, among English civilians, was one of the most accurate and painstaking of all past official authorities on Indian customs, and his words may be implicitly relied on. He writes as follows:—

"Whenever, in fact, marriage is the custom, the bride and bridegroom do not come together till a second ceremony called *Muklawa* has been performed; till then the bride lives as a virgin in her father's house. This second ceremony is separated from the actual wedding by an interval of three, five, seven, nine, or eleven years, and the girl's parents fix the time for it. Thus it often happens that the earlier in life marriage takes place, the later cohabitation begins."

This statement of Sir Denzil Ibbetson is confirmed by the Census Commissioner of the United Provinces for 1921. These provinces are one of the centres of orthodox Hinduism, and therefore his statement may be taken as typical of Hinduism elsewhere. "Marriage," he states, "among the Hindus means no more than irrevocable betrothal. The parties do not begin to live together immediately after the ceremony, but after the lapse of an indefinite period, generally not less than one and not more than five years."

The reason why Hindu parents are often in such a hurry to get their children married is very simple. The caste divisions have become so elaborate that now they number well over a thousand when all the subdivisions are reckoned in. This limits the area of choice for marriage to a very considerable degree, because intercaste marriages are rare up to the present time. Therefore the father is anxious to obtain a suitable match for his daughter and cannot brook delay. For it is commonly regarded as a social disgrace in India to have a daughter reach womanhood without marriage, though it needs at once to be added that the rigidity of such a customary belief is breaking down under the national impulse.

Four things would immensely accelerate the movement towards that abolition of child marriage which every reasonable man in India desires.

(1) The first of these is the encouragement of intermarriages between subdivisions in the same caste. This is now being advocated at every caste meeting. Whenever (to give one instance) there is a general gathering of the large Kayastha Community, the first resolution that is put forward and passed unanimously is the necessity of breaking down the subdivisions within the caste as a whole with regard to marriage. It is pointed out that the evils of child marriage itself, and the further evil that goes with it of claiming a very high sum from the father of the bride, would all be diminished if the area of choice was widened by the recognition of all caste marriages within the one caste as legitimate and by the breaking down of all subdivisions within the caste.

(2) In the second place it is worthy of special note that those who have come under the influence of the great national awakening advocate inter-

marriage between the different castes. Mahatma Gandhi has given his sanction to the marriage of his youngest son Devidas outside his own caste altogether; and no marriage in recent years has been more happy and popular than this. What would have raised a storm a generation ago has been welcomed to-day. Every villager in India gets to know what Mahatma Gandhi does; and an action like this about marriage is widely canvassed. It marks a new era in Hindu religion.

(3) The third remedy against child marriage is the breaking down of the superstition already mentioned that a father commits a mortal sin if he allows his daughter to grow up unmarried. Here the whole attitude towards family and social life is rapidly changing. The large number of openings for medical and educational service that can be filled only by unmarried women is being slowly recognized by Hindu society generally. Parents are beginning to take pride in allowing their daughters to remain unmarried in order to serve the community. Thus to have a vocation in some noble field of service is regarded as a perfectly valid cause for the daughter remaining unmarried. There are also young men who deeply respect those who have spent their earlier years in such vocations. They prefer to marry at what in India has been considered a comparatively advanced age, and they look for a wife who will be a true helpmeet both in age and education.

I am fully aware that the two last considerations hardly as yet do more than touch the fringe of the *village* problem. For in the village these vocations are as yet not easily found, and intercaste marriage is too bold a step for the conservative and illiterate villager to undertake. Superstition stands in the way, and custom prevails. The change in village customs must to us appear almost incredibly slow. Nevertheless a movement has begun which gathers fresh impetus every year.

Here the national movement under the religious leadership of Mahatma Gandhi has brought in the new motive of patriotism, and the widespread effect of this has struck every one who has been watching modern India with sympathetic eyes. For this national awakening has reached the remotest villages, and what Mahatma Gandhi does is talked of everywhere and becomes a new sanction to millions in favour of what they wished to do but were prevented by evil custom from undertaking.

(4) In the end, the greatest of all considerations which will go to prevent these child marriages in the future will be the spread of girls' education. It is here where the Government of India, by its meagre grants, has been most to blame. With popular Governments now in office in the provinces the rate of progress will be immensely accelerated.

While I was in British Guiana and Trinidad living in the midst of the Hindu community out there, which had given up all caste restrictions, I found to my surprise that the evil of child marriage still prevailed in certain districts. But wherever the education of girls had gone forward and schools had been provided the number of child marriages remarkably decreased. Those who had most at heart the complete abolition of this evil custom of child marriage were convinced that with the spread of girls' education it would disappear. The facts and figures to which they pointed were significant; and though the reform may come more slowly in village India, there can be little doubt that the same remedy of girls' education will produce similar results.

There is one difficult and formidable subject with which Miss Mayo deals at some length in her books—the spread of venereal disease. Her statements are general, and she gives no reliable figures or statistics. In carrying on social reform work I have been obliged to enquire into the evidence of this malady. From personal enquiries, carried on over a large number of years, two facts appear to me to be fairly certain. (1) The larger towns of India have been very badly infected. Every medical officer who has had to deal with the city problem has come to this conclusion. (2) In most parts of India the contrary appears to be the condition of the country districts. Since the vast proportion of the people of India live in the villages, it seems to me fairly certain therefore that over the whole of India the percentage of infected people is low.

At the same time the danger of the infection spreading to the country from the towns is every year increasing. This is due especially to the migratory habits of Indian industrial labour, which congregates from the villages into the larger towns and then returns to the villages after a season. Herein lies a serious danger.

One interesting piece of positive evidence came to me in the course of an enquiry which I published in a report. At the hospital at Namirembe in Uganda Dr. Cook, the superintendent, gave me his own written testimony, based on over twenty years' experience, that the infection among his Indian patients was far lower than that among the Europeans or the Baganda. This was with regard to Indians living for the most part a life of partial separation from their own families, the latter having remained in India. He gave me verbally a rough estimate, and the lower proportion of infection on the Indian side was very marked indeed.

All that I have gathered as a social worker would lead me very seriously to doubt Miss Mayo's vague statements about this disease in India itself. It appears to have come to India from the West, and to have been prevalent in Europe long before India was infected. Since Europe and America are far more urbanized than India, it seems to me almost certain that in this matter India has not reached the high incidence of infection that has become common in the West.

While thus pointing out the discrepancies in Miss Mayo's account of the Indian situation, I do not at all wish to imply that the marriage age is as yet satisfactory, or that the spread of venereal disease is a negligible matter. Child marriages with actual consummation are still much too common, and their results are always deplorable. Even where there is comparatively little suffering involved there is a pitifully enfeebled offspring. Disgraceful marriages between old men and young girls (owing chiefly to the barrier against widow remarriage) still continue to occur. They are not yet condemned sufficiently by healthy public opinion, though even here things are rapidly improving. A short time ago such a marriage on the part of a social worker himself called forth an immediate outburst of condemnation. Social reformers, one and all, would welcome eagerly every attempt made to hasten the day of reform. But such reform is only retarded where facts are exaggerated and misstated. Nothing can do more harm than to create resentment by unfair and inaccurate special pleading.

One of the chapters in Miss Mayo's book, which will evoke pity and sympathy in the West, is that which describes the agonies of child-birth due to very early marriage. Neither I personally nor those who endorse my views would defend for a moment cruelties of this kind whenever they are practised. They are evils to be removed at the first possible moment, and the public conscience greatly needs rousing in these matters, so that reform may be speedy and also wisely directed. The facts of suffering in this special matter in India have been recognized for a long time past, and very important and necessary steps, such as the training of midwives, or *dais*, have already been taken, with the strength of public opinion behind them to make them a success.

Most of us recognize that there has been much lethargy to overcome and much indifference. It is only when sweeping generalizations are made, based on hospital cases, that the time comes to protest in the name of truth against a gross perversion of facts.

For in our deep sympathy with the young mother, with whose pain and peril in her first child-birth every humane person must have profound compassion, we shall not help the cause of truth by exaggeration as to the amount of suffering that normally takes place. There are abnormal cases of malformation where this pain of child-birth must be terrible beyond words, because no relief is at hand from modern surgery and anaesthetics. But taking India as a whole—the India of countless villages, of open-air life and country habits of living, of hardy primitive existence, unspoilt by the artificial habits of the towns—it is not surprising to find, as any impartial observer will notice, how natural and simple child-birth usually is, and how quickly mothers resume their ordinary occupations. The villagers of India have learnt their own daily lessons. Undoubtedly these age-long habits of theirs in some very important matters have got to be drastically revised. New lessons of hygiene have to be taught. But normally the villagers are able to perform these central functions of human life with but little adventitious aid from without. Long centuries of past experience, wherein doctors in the modern sense of the term were not available, have obliged them to practise self-help. The fittest survive. Those who have proved their fitness have themselves discovered many ways of making human life comparatively tolerable. Nevertheless there are instances, as I have said, of malformation which cannot be dealt with in ordinary ways; and here the suffering could be largely diminished if modern medical and surgical methods were made available.

Certainly, when we see the village women in many parts of India, with their erect bearing, their grace of motion, their laughter and their songs, as they perform their daily tasks, we have the clear sense of sufferings lightly borne. Only the sting of hunger remains, over very large areas indeed, causing a weakness, a misery, a pain, that no improved methods of domestic hygiene can cure, unless along with them the rate of daily earnings is raised, and thus proper nourishment is placed within the poor man's compass. It is to these districts, such as the half-starved areas of Orissa, Bihar, and Western Bengal, that our sympathies ought to be directed. Here, very often, there is no smile and happy laughter, but only grinding misery and want from one year's end to the other.

If these writers from the West had actually obtained at first hand intimate knowledge of this village life, through living for long years in its midst and reviewing it in all its homely aspects, they would have found that much the most serious factor in delaying progress and recuperation is the grinding poverty of the poor. Diseases of every kind, and especially malaria and dysentery, are apt to get a fatal hold on the physique of those who suffer from lifelong malnutrition. This deficiency of diet causes much of the misery which these books luridly depict. The fundamental remedy which is being emphasized to-day is a diet that does not leave the nervous system starved and reduce the vitality to such a point that there is no resistance to infection. The high mortality in maternity cases has its root cause often in this direction, making child-birth more than usually difficult and causing complications.

I can well understand that I am risking the inference being left by my words, that I am making light of acute human suffering of a very unbearable kind, and taking the sting out of the stern warnings which Nature gives, so that they fail to have their full effect of goading the public conscience of India into concerted action. I would grant that a goad may be needed; that life in a tropical climate becomes terribly apathetic, so that things fall back again and no permanent benefit results. But to goad the public conscience effectively is like an act of surgery. And surgery needs a very skilful hand. It cannot be performed in a hurried moment by a flying visitor who has mixed truth and falsehood together. Nothing in the world does more harm than to wound sensitive public feeling by harsh incisions made in wrong places.

Surely in such matters there is a profound meaning in the old saying, "Charity begins at home." After all, each country, up to a certain point, knows best through its own age-long experience how to solve its own problems. Hasty, ill-considered interference from the outside, however generously intended, often adds to the sum of human suffering instead of diminishing it. Even among the primitive tribes of Central Africa it has been found necessary to take into account crude customs which have a survival value rather than ruthlessly to sweep them all away. Here in India, where custom has gone so deep and human society can trace back its own recorded history for thousands of years, the work of an iconoclast leads often to greater evils than those that are attacked. Least of all is it possible for any traveller, with complete ignorance of the languages of the country and extremely scanty knowledge in other directions, to attempt all in a moment to set things right by a few harsh sentences harshly written.

Chapter 11

WOMEN'S RIGHTS

ONE Act of legislation, called the "Sarda Marriage Act," which has recently been amended by the strengthening of some of its clauses, shows us that legislative enactment is still imperative if the verdict of public opinion is to be ratified and confirmed. This brings us directly to further important questions concerning the rights of women under Hinduism which badly need to be revised and brought up to date in accordance with the spirit of the times, if Hindu society is to make progress while everything around is passing through a revolutionary upheaval. Changes are also needed with regard to the rights of women under Islamic law in India, but these cannot be dealt with in this chapter.

One of the greatest evils of the past, in Hindu customary law as it has gradually been formulated in India, has been the complete subordination of women. The law of inheritance weighs very heavily indeed to-day against the rights of the women of the family when they need to be protected. Though the duties of the head of the family imply that the women are to be cared for with every consideration, yet this mandatory method does not ensure any legal security, and therefore instances of shameful neglect and cruel suffering occur, which have no remedy under Hindu law as it stands to-day.

Now that women themselves in India are entering the Councils and even holding office as Cabinet Ministers, it can hardly be long before legislation will be brought forward in the different provinces correcting some of these anomalies. What has happened in other countries will soon occur in India, and we may well hope that the time will not be far distant when great changes will be made. The National Congress declaration of fundamental rights gives to women absolute equality with men in every sphere of life: but that ideal is as yet far ahead in the future. The following picture has been given in a leading periodical, on its "Woman's Page," dealing with conditions as they are in Hindu India to-day.

"Dispossessed at birth and disinherited throughout life, the Hindu woman is expected to thrive on a precarious state of existence! In fact, there is nothing by way of legal rights which makes her in any way economically independent; her subservience is just as complete, dowry or no dowry. It is obvious that the *stridhan* (dowry) can in no sense be made a justification for her not having the right to inherit property.

"All her personal laws, it is very clear, were framed to suit conditions very dissimilar to the conditions in which she finds herself to-day. The Hindu rulers of India were conquered by the Muhammadans, who no doubt brought with them laws of inheritance definitely more liberal to women; but whatever changes they brought about did not affect the personal lives of Indian women as a whole. The Muhammadan rulers were later on succeeded by the British. The contact with the British has resulted, at least outwardly, in a partial breakdown of the old, inelastic order. But this appears to have made very little impression on the archaic laws of the land, particularly as they relate to women's personal rights.

"The women of India, who were disinherited and made dependents of men, remain very much in the same state in spite of the spread of education and the gradual disappearance of the *purdah*. The average woman of India to-day continues to be, in the eyes of the law, a dependent, a social inferior.

"Unless the laws of inheritance and marriage are radically changed, the general mass of women in India can never become self-reliant nor will they learn to respect themselves. The time is therefore ripe for radical changes to be made. The most urgently needed reforms are these:—

(1) Granting women the right to inherit property.
(2) Making all marriage monogamous.
(3) Granting of divorce.
(4) Abolition of dowry by law.
(5) Stiffening of the Child Marriage Act.

"Should these reforms be made possible, the whole aspect of things will change. Women in India would at last have an opportunity to develop into adult human beings."

Already the Child Marriage Act has been strengthened, and in many cases to-day the Civil Marriage Act is now employed under which monogamy is legally recognized and women are allowed to inherit property. But there are still difficulties in the way which prevent this form of marriage being freely utilized *along with* a religious ceremony.

With regard to the life lived by the women of India in our own day, I can speak with some experience; for there is not a province of India where I have not shared their confidence and heard at first hand their story. As a man of religion, I have also been asked very often, when I have gone from place to place, to address those women who were still in purdah. Indian women themselves have thus told me about the hardships and cruel wrongs from which they suffer, and I do not write from hearsay only.

It may well be true that I do not know the technical details of the marriage law or the law of inheritance, and there are many other social questions relating to women which are far beyond me; but I *do* know and understand with a loving heart the bad effects of many parts of the customary law, as Indians have themselves explained it to me, and I can easily see how completely out of date it is at the present time.

One of the greatest hindrances to any change has been the natural reluctance of British rulers to interfere in matters of religion. But the large new powers which are already placed in the hands of the people of the country to reform their own laws in the different provinces will surely hasten the time when these injustices will be brought to an end. Then the Indian woman will take her place at last side by side with man as an equal in every respect.

One very happy omen, which seems to show quite clearly that this day is soon approaching, has been the remarkable promptness wherewith, almost without opposition, the higher posts in the professions and also in the Government itself are being thrown open to women. That which had involved a prolonged and bitter struggle in Great Britain and other progressive countries has been freely surrendered in India. No doubt the women who struggled so courageously and with such wonderful persistence in Great Britain were the pioneers. Indian women owe them a debt of gratitude which can never be repaid. They opened a door to reform which before had been closed. So when India's turn came to advance there was hardly anywhere prolonged hostility on the part of the men who held the reins of power. While in the days of Pandita Ramabai the conflict was incredibly severe, in these latter days the rights which women have demanded all along have been almost eagerly conceded. This concession has not been merely nominal. Probably the only part of India where such a sweeping statement would have to be modified would be the north-west.

All this has happened since the war. When I came out to India at the beginning of the century there was no sign anywhere that I can recollect of the amazing advance we have seen since. Woman was right in the background, almost out of sight, in public life. But now, with a grace and dignity that has impressed every one, she has come into the foreground of the picture.

The remarkably beneficial effects of the changes which have taken place have been recognized by all. Municipal life has been lifted to a higher standard of care for the poor and destitute, the weak and helpless. The extraordinarily difficult and uphill battle against insanitation in the home has been carried forward till one position after another has been gained. The prevention of disease within the domestic circle, especially in the care of children, has been rendered more effective. Maternity help has been made available through the disbursement of public funds, where before great suffering and even death had frequently occurred owing to the neglect of medical and surgical aid and the want of proper nourishment.

These things have been made possible simply because leading Indian women have not only freely entered municipal life, but have become members of legislative councils. What is more, this rapid progress that has already been made is likely to be still further accelerated as time goes on. Already a woman has been chosen as a Cabinet Minister with remarkably good results, and the day seems not far distant when at least one of the provinces of India will be governed and administered by a woman.

Thank God! We can now look back and recognize with a grateful heart some of these immensely promising and potent changes which have already taken place. Yet we are but at the beginning of things, and those who have been all along the principal leaders of the Women's Movement in India have warned us again and again that even now the villages themselves are still in a great measure isolated from the new, throbbing life at the centre, and that it is in the villages that the greatest work of all awaits accomplishment if the masses of poor people are to be reached and their sufferings relieved.

How much still remains to be done may be gathered from one of the most remarkable utterances that has recently been made by the Rajkumari Amrit Kaur, Vice-President of the National Y.W.C.A. and President of the All-India Women's Conference. She began by saying that every woman ought to be a public servant if she rightly understood the function of womanhood in society. As one who had a profound belief in womankind, she was convinced that the baffling problems of the world to-day could be solved if only women would realize their responsibility.

"What is the contribution women can make?" she asked. "What can we do, and how are we to do it?" The answer was to be found when women understood what was their rightful place in the social order. "Why is it," she asked again, "that everywhere inequalities exist between men and women? Who is to blame?" The answer usually given was that man, being physically stronger than woman, had to be the protector and wage-earner, and therefore he had the right himself to build up the social order without consulting woman's interests. He certainly had done it, and in consequence great inequalities persisted. But the true reason why such inequalities went on was because women had submitted and taken this state of things as a matter of course. The exploited are to blame for allowing themselves to be exploited. It was not the civic and political franchise alone which would give women the place they should have in the social order. It was only as women shared the moral and spiritual values of life, and thus had something higher to contribute to the social order, that they could take their rightful place in it. Women must stress moral values without fear, and the supremacy of service without the reward of personal gain.

"What can women individually and collectively do?" she asked. The number of educated women in India was so small in proportion to the uneducated and ignorant that no woman who had received education could remain idle. Each one must play her part in dispelling the darkness that shrouded this great land. But the educated lived chiefly in towns, while the real India was to be found in the villages, where the poverty-stricken mass of India's population passed their existence. Many educated Indian women, especially in the north, had adopted false standards of living. For the sake of serving the poor, educated women must become poor in spirit and must adopt simplicity in their mode of life.

They must learn to spend only what they really needed, and the rest must be held as a trust and be given to help the poor. To do this should not be regarded as a sacrifice. When women came in close contact with the poor and lived among them, they would not find it difficult to reduce their own wants. There would not be any real lessening of beauty; for beauty was to be found chiefly in simplicity and purity.

It was women who were needed to work in the villages even more than men. They could help the villagers to understand the beauty of cleanliness, to discipline the children, to know more about food values, and to practise cottage industries.

There was the same need in the slums of the great cities. Superstition, untouchability, and lavish spending should be courageously challenged wherever they were found. Women should help in the prohibition campaign by providing something better to take the place that drink had in the past in the lives of the poor people. Women should help to create the conviction that child marriage was an evil custom, for without such a conviction legislation could do little. Women could also do much to encourage the use of hand-made articles by care in selecting what they allowed in their own homes, and so avoid the evils which had come through over-mechanization.

Women could heal the communal disunity, which was a canker eating into the vitals of Indian national life. This communal feeling was not found among women as it was among men. It was not found also in women's organizations. Communal friction was not really religious in origin, but a conflict of material interests. Women must be willing and courageous enough to go into the heart of the communal riots when they occurred and say to the men, "We will not have it!" They must even be ready to sacrifice their lives in this cause.

Women must also raise the professional standards of medicine and law, so that all in these professions should seek to give their service without fear or favour and without seeking mere personal gain. Why should politics be a dirty game? Here also women could set the ideal of service above every personal advantage, and thus make politics clean.

Last of all, women should think internationally. If the countries of the world could only get closer to one another spiritually as they have been doing geographically, all might be well. But everywhere there were aggression and exploitation and countries torn asunder. The women of the world must unite. They must learn to say, not "My country right or wrong," but "My world"; and the women of Italy, Germany, and Japan must join also. All of them desired peace, but what were they really doing? Their past helplessness must go. They had to take their stand against aggression and exploitation wherever it was to be found. What would happen if women should refuse to work in munition factories or take part in gas-mask parades? The only way to save a world that was running headlong to its own destruction was to adopt the creed of love, truth, and non-violence.

A section here needs to be added about the purdah system, which has done untold harm during the past centuries wherever it has gained a firm and rigid hold upon the minds of the people. For it has degraded the whole idea of woman and prevented her from ever attaining that complete equality with man which is the National Congress ideal.

Purdah, by its cramping and confining atmosphere, kills both body and soul among the ordinary rank and file of those who practise it. Supremely great and noble women have been able to rise above it and to exercise an influence behind the veil of seclusion that has astonished mankind: but even here the genius of these rare souls would have found far greater scope if the veil had been removed. Therefore, in their case also the tragedy has been hardly less lamentable.

While condemning the present state of things, it is necessary to make clear to those outside India that to-day in almost every province the purdah system is beginning to break down. The weight of social opinion is being shifted to the other side of the scale, and the balance now points towards its speedy removal.

Even in the past, in a sub-continent like India, its practice was extremely limited. It was confined to certain parts of the country, and also to certain ranks of society. Strangely enough, to our Western mode of thinking, one of the chief difficulties of removing the purdah comes from the fact that it is assumed to be a mark of high rank and respectability. Among the poorer classes, which form the vast majority of the population, it is rarely practised, and in large areas of India it has never been introduced at all. Village women have on the whole been free from it. In the extreme north-west it is still regarded as a necessity among certain ranks of society.

The Indian nation which is now being born—including Muslims as well as Hindus, Parsees, and Christians—has set its face steadily against it. Here again, Mahatma Gandhi and Rabindranath Tagore have been its strongest opponents. In addition, every national leader of importance is against the system, even though some of them may find difficulty as yet, within their own social or religious area, in advocating its entire removal. It is now recognized that its effect has been most harmful to the full development of Indian womanhood on the lines of equality and freedom, and also on the lines of good health and physical vigour. The most convincing proofs of its harmfulness have been those put forward by medical science. Since the time when tuberculosis began to be a scourge in India, as well as in England, the confined atmosphere of the zenana has proved to be one of the most deadly breeding grounds of the disease.

Thus it is recognized on every hand that the time has come to bring the purdah system to an end. It is difficult to show, in the brief compass of a book of this kind, how the abolition of the purdah system will have its own beneficial effect in preventing child marriage and other social evils; but those who are most enthusiastic in helping to bring about its removal have put up a very strong case to show that not only physical evils will be diminished, but social and moral evils will disappear also.

Legislation will be finally needed when public opinion has been fully formed and the nation has made up its mind. Along with the new responsibility in the provinces the power of legislation by consent, even on such difficult matters as this, will be rendered more easy. This goes to show the truth of the saying that is often repeated by Indian leaders, that the revolution which has now begun in India is not only political but also social and moral.

NOTE

A revolt among many of the leading members of the Hindu community against the serious evils connected with child marriage has led to a reconsideration of the whole problem of those rare cases where the husband, who has been already married to a child wife, repudiates her and contracts a second marriage with one who is educated in modern ways and habits. Legislation is being proposed which, if passed, would ensure monogamy on the one hand and the right of the wife to divorce her husband, in certain extreme instances, such as that of complete desertion, on the other. Two proposed Bills are quoted below.

Dr. Deshmukh's "Hindu Women's Right of Divorce Bill" reads as follows:—

Whereas it is expedient to give a Right of Divorce to Hindu women under certain circumstances, it is enacted as follows:—

(1) This Act may be called the Hindu Women's Right of Divorce Act of 1938.

It shall apply to the whole of India (British). It shall come into force on ——.

(2) Notwithstanding any custom or law to the contrary a married Hindu woman shall be entitled to claim a divorce from her husband under the following circumstances:—

If her husband acquires impotency, any time after the marriage, which is incurable;

or, If her husband changes his religion;

or, If her husband marries a woman while the first marriage is in force;

or, If her husband has deserted her for a continuous period of three years.

The Hon. Seth Govindlal S. Motilal's Bill reads thus:—

Whereas it is expedient to forbid and declare illegal a marriage contracted by a Hindu with another woman in the lifetime of his wife, it is hereby enacted as follows:—

(1) (i) This Act may be called the Hindu Monogamous Act of 1938.

(ii) It extends to the whole of British India and shall come into force on such date as it receives the assent of the Governor-General.

(2) Notwithstanding any rule of Hindu Law or custom, contrary or inconsistent with this Act, a marriage contracted

by a Hindu with another woman in the lifetime of his wife, shall be void, and the provisions of Section 494 and 495. (Bigamy sections) of the Indian Penal Code shall apply to such a marriage,

Provided that this section shall not apply to a marriage contracted by a Hindu where, by law or custom, dissolution of marriage is permissible and has been granted by competent authority.

(3) The provisions of this Act shall apply to a Hindu even after his conversion to another religion.

These are merely two out of a number of Bills that are being already proposed both in the Provincial Councils and also in the Central Assembly. Just at the time that this note is being written, Mrs. Subbaroyan, the wife of a Minister of the Madras Government and a member of the Central Assembly, has given notice of a similar Bill for All-India to prevent polygamy.

While any such legislation is likely to meet with the strongest opposition from orthodox Hindus and may have to wait a long time before it finally becomes the law of the whole of India, like the Sarda Act, it is a welcome sign of the times that measures of this character should be put forward by leading Hindus themselves as a remedy for the grievous sufferings to Indian womanhood which the present customary law involves. When, at last, a new law for the whole of India is passed, it is likely to have two sections:—

(1) The making of monogamy the only form of marriage under Hindu law.

(2) The legal sanction of divorce in certain extreme cases.

Chapter 12

THE DEPRESSED CLASSES

INDIAN Nationalism stands or falls by its attitude with regard to what Mahatma Gandhi has often called the "sin of untouchability." The origins of this evil have been already discussed while describing the caste system in India.

The progress which has already been made towards its removal may be partly measured from the fact that the word "untouchable" has now been dropped, and the euphemism *Harijan* (meaning "children of God") has been adopted instead. The Government now uses the neutral term "Scheduled Castes." But unless something far more than a mere change of name takes place, their lot may not be permanently altered, and every effort is now being made to bring about permanent improvement. The whole monstrous system has to be brought to an end whereby they are still penalized in every direction and treated as if they were subhuman.

Educated India is endeavouring rapidly to cast out once and for all this pernicious evil in the same way that it is attacking "purdah" and "child marriage." It aims at nothing less than the entire removal of this great blot from Indian life in the course of the present generation. To accomplish this would indeed be a miracle, but it is not impossible. The system is one of those bad relics of the past which must forthwith be abolished if India is to hold up her head among the nations. Mahatma Gandhi long ago saw this clearly and took into his own family one of these "untouchable" children, treating her in every way as his own daughter. Whenever she has accompanied him on his tours he has insisted on her being taken into the homes of high-caste people; and if on any occasion, at some town or village gathering, the outcastes, or untouchables, are seated on the ground apart, he at once notices it, and invariably goes and takes his own seat among them. This puts the orthodox to shame, and when he invites them to come over to his side they consent to do so.

"So long," Mahatma Gandhi declares, "as untouchability disfigures Hinduism, so long do I hold the attainment of Swaraj to be an utter impossibility. Supposing it were a gift descending from Downing Street, that gift would be a curse upon this land, if we did not get rid of *this* curse!"

Thus very gradually, but surely, changes are taking place; for compared with all the other moral forces in India put together the effect of Mahatma Gandhi's personality is the greatest. It makes no difference whether he visits the Muslim villages in East and North Bengal, or the Travancore Hindu villages in the extreme south, where Hindu orthodoxy has long had its greatest hold, the effect of his presence is felt throughout the length and breadth of the country-side wherever he passes. I have accompanied him on these journeys, and am writing about the facts which I have witnessed and taken part in, not of things merely heard at second hand.

How great is the urgency for this reform, which only one with a spiritual dynamic like Mahatma Gandhi could carry through, can hardly be imagined by those who do not know India from the inside. A story of what happened in Travancore may illustrate best the immediate need. I had gone down there, by request of Mahatma Gandhi, at a time when he was ill and could not travel about. At one place near Tiruvalla a gathering was held in the open at which more than two thousand "untouchables" were present. Even though I was wearing Indian dress, they shrank back at first as though I might treat them with harshness. But Mr. K. K. Kuruvilla, who was the head of the Mar Thoma Seminary, was with me, and he managed to reassure them. Then at last they pressed round me, making prostration on the ground before me; and thus in an abject manner they implored my help.

Their misery was beyond words, and the story of their suffering was heart-rending to hear. Their landlords used them merely as serfs of the soil, paying them a casual pittance of less than twopence a day whenever they took work from them. In this part of India the Syrian Christians, who form a large section of the population, had kept apart from these depressed people with hardly less aloofness than the high-caste Hindus. Such an evil grip had the "sin of untouchability" got upon all classes! Inveterate custom had settled upon the Christians almost as much as upon the caste people.

That was one of the greatest tragedies in the past. But, thank God, all this is changing with extraordinary rapidity. When I asked whether such aloofness would be usual among Syrian Christians at the present time, I was told that it could not happen. They had learnt at last the lesson which Christ Himself had taught them.

At one place near Trivandrum, on a later occasion, I had gone forward by myself to see the foul condition inside a hovel where a family of Cherumas was living. When I drew near, however, the poor mother, holding a tiny baby in her arm, with two young children at her side, suddenly appeared and gave a pitiful cry of horror and alarm. Though I had approached with a heart filled with pity, she imagined I had come there to strike her! Inhumanity, centuries old, had reduced her and her children to that panic-stricken level of abject misery.

Stories like this could be multiplied from my own experience in many parts of India.[1] If the national movement had not come like an overwhelming tide to sweep all this away, things in India would still be intolerable. But the fact which has now become patent is this: that never in the whole of Indian history has such a nation-wide effort been started to get rid of this cruel evil, once and for all, and to treat these depressed millions as brothers and equals. This is no political expedient, but a true moral

[1] See Chapter 4, pp. 54 and 55.

revolution, in which the women of India have taken a principal part.

In that very State of Travancore, which I have chosen for my illustrations because it is the worst in all India in this respect, there has been such an outstanding advance that the whole situation has altered. The Maharaja and the Maharani have issued an edict declaring all the State temples, over fifteen hundred in number, to be made fully open to the Harijans (untouchables) on exactly the same conditions as to the caste Hindus. This proclamation has gone much further than the opening of the State temples; for other temples also, endowed by private persons and held by private trusts, have been opened. This has happened, not only in Travancore, but also in other parts of the south, where orthodoxy had before been most rigidly established. In the northern provinces temples had already been opened in large numbers; for this evil has never had the same grip on the north. But this blow to narrow orthodoxy in the extreme south has resounded all over the country.

The religious impetus which this has given has been rightly described as a new reformation within Hinduism itself. With a thoroughness that seemed impossible only a few years ago, one barrier after another has been broken down; and the reform is all the more sweeping because it has come from within and has not been imposed from without. Even the Maharaja of Travancore's Edict came at the end of a long preparation by thousands of devoted workers under the leadership of Mahatma Gandhi.[1] It set the seal on efforts that had already been made and found an immediate response in the hearts of the people who were waiting and praying for such an act to be performed.

In the midst of the almost universal rejoicing that such a victory over the evil of "untouchability" has caused it may seem unnecessary to draw attention to the accounts that are given of the "untouchables" in various books which have recently emanated from the West, but the neglect to refer to the indigenous efforts made by Indians themselves to overcome this evil has shown how little the true situation has been grasped by their authors. In this kind of literature, the Harijans have been pitted against the educated classes at the very time when the latter, under Mahatma Gandhi's leadership, have been doing everything in their power, and almost beyond their power, to remove the evil. This political use of the "untouchables," as a weapon to strike at the politically educated classes, is a thoroughly demoralizing expedient; and books that are written explaining that "if the British rule were withdrawn from India, everything would fall back again, and the depressed classes would be treated as badly as they were of old," do not really face the facts. For the simple truth is this: that it would be as difficult for things to go back now, after the social revolution that has taken place, as it would be difficult for woman in India to go back into her old position of subordina-

[1] See Chapter 4, pp. 54 and 55.

tion. The millions of the depressed classes are themselves in open revolt, and this revolt is being strongly encouraged by caste Hindus who have emancipated themselves from the evil bondage of caste in these directions. The movement forward has begun. It has already swept the old landmarks away, and the tide to-day is advancing more rapidly than ever.

One thing further needs to be said with the greatest tenderness and care. In the past, when the conscience of Hindu India was dead on this tremendous issue, and the inhuman treatment of the pariahs was at its worst, the Christian missions in south India revealed what the power of sympathy and love could effect. This was, perhaps, the most convincing testimony to the influence of the Christian Faith. Many thousands of these depressed classes were rescued from a lifelong degradation which had sunk almost below the human level. They were changed into men and women who gained the respect even of those who had treated them so badly. There was no opposition at that time offered by Hindus to such rescue work. There was also little or no attempt among Hindus in the south to reform their own social order from within. All this, I believe, would be granted by any impartial historian of the nineteenth century in India.

But things have now entirely changed. Hinduism, with inner faith and hope and courage, is reforming itself. It is seeking to accomplish over the whole of India that "rescue" work which was begun by the Christian missions in confined areas more than a century ago. At last it is offering to these millions of outcastes an honourable place within the social order. Splendid acts of sincere reformation have already been made. The seats allotted to these classes in the provincial councils have been nearly doubled, with the consent of the caste Hindus themselves. The temples, as I have related, have been opened over a large part of the country. The whole outlook is changed radically from what it was a century or even sixty years ago.

Is it possible now for the Christian missions to welcome this advance, from within Hinduism, as a true movement of the Spirit of the Living God? The whole future of Christianity in India appears to me to depend on the answer to that question. Is not Christ, who warmly welcomed the acts of the good Samaritan and the Roman centurion and the Greek Syro-Phoenician woman, teaching us in a similar manner to welcome every act of faith which Hindus to-day are making to raise the poor and oppressed? Even if it is not done consciously in His name, will He not say, "Ye did it unto Me"? If only Christians can be generous to-day in recognizing the good work that Hinduism is now doing among these very classes, then there will be a real hope of advance all along the line. There is no room for rivalry or distrust where so many millions of lives are at stake.

Those of us who are seeking to follow Christ as our example have to remember that we have our own evil past to overcome, owing to the "colour problem," and that Hinduism is not alone in being called upon to face this wrong done to a depressed people. We have seen in South Africa a deliberate policy pursued whereby complete segregation is being attempted, social and political, between the white and coloured races—even between Christian and Christian. We are told that "racial segregation" is a fundamental principle which must be carried out both in Church and State. Those who profess to worship Christ as Lord openly deny Him in this manner. They practise what is virtually "untouchability" within the boundaries of the Christian Church. What is happening to-day in South Africa has already come about in the south of the United States of America. There also the colour bar has been established within the Church of Christ, and Christians refuse to worship side by side with their fellow Christians of another colour. While these two countries represent flagrant breaches of the law of Christian brotherhood, there are also all over the world those who call themselves Christians, and yet hold these very "racial" doctrines which Christ Himself condemned. Even in India, as we have seen, the Church of Christ is by no means guiltless in this respect. "Untouchability" has crept in there also, especially in the south. Therefore it is supremely necessary for Christians themselves to put their own house in order.

This unsolved "colour" question in the United States and also in South Africa, where racial segregation continues; the ghetto system in Eastern Europe;

the depressed classes who still suffer in Japan; the whole peonage system in Central and South America; the forced labour in many parts of Africa—all these things, and much else besides, stand or fall together. They really form one issue, which the West as well as the East must set out to solve. The West must not try to pull the mote out of India's eye while the beam remains in its own eye.

For the so-called "untouchables" of India, as we have seen, are the relics of racial and political conquests made many centuries ago. They carry on into the present very ancient colour prejudices whose origin has now been entirely forgotten. These struggles are centuries old, and they will not disappear in a day. But those who represent the National Movement of India desire to tell to other countries, without any reservation, that educated Indians on their part are determined to abolish all such dominations of one race by another, or of one colour over another, as far as lies in their power. They have felt too deeply the misery of subjection themselves to have any desire to impose it on the weak. In the Declaration of Rights which has been passed at many Congress sessions this has been made quite clear.

They do not defend for a single moment "untouchability" in India. But they claim at the same time that the West should not be too ready with its own condemnation. They also demand from the Labour Movement in South Africa and elsewhere that there should be no barrier against the admission of Indian workers along with other races, on equal terms, on the basis of equal pay for equal work, and a minimum wage which shall apply to all races alike.

If it be asked further by what method the abolition of "untouchability" and the removal of other social evils of a similar character in India may best be attained, the following answer may be given in general terms.

India is essentially a peaceful country, with its heart set on peace. Now and then crowds may be lashed to madness by momentary excitement, as the occasional religious riots have shown; but the instinct of the Indian villager, whether Hindu or Muslim, is to remain attached to the soil in peace.

It follows from this that the man who speaks to the soul of India must speak, not by appeals to violence, but with moral authority based upon a saintly and ascetic life. The appeal must be personal and embodied in a person, because the thousands of Indian villages, and the millions of the villagers, can only be reached directly and simply by these personal methods. Thus true social reforms must be embodied and made visible in an individual, universally loved and revered, in order to obtain the full emotional urge from myriads of human hearts that may carry it on to permanent success.

This obviously means in practice that the presence of one gifted and deeply religious soul, such as Mahatma Gandhi, whose name has reached to the heart of every "untouchable" in India and is almost worshipped by them, is an infinitely greater power for good than all the legislation in the world. Legal powers may be needed later to register the social changes which have taken place and carry them into permanent effect. But the central influence and inspiration is the man of God.

Chapter 13

THE POVERTY OF INDIA

SOME of the princes and wealthy men of India have done a great disservice to their mother country by flaunting their wealth in a vulgar and tawdry manner in the fashionable hotels of the West. They have given the idea by doing so that India is a fabulously wealthy country. This view of India, which dates back to very ancient times, has become almost a tradition. It was immensely strengthened and exaggerated in the eighteenth century, when freebooters and adventurers brought back from a conquered and oppressed people the loot in such quantities that it corrupted the whole political life of Great Britain and nearly led to a moral disaster of the first order.

Even to-day the same tradition continues under other forms; for the exploitation still goes on by those who in business methods and capitalist enterprise are using the weapons of the strong against the weak.

Dr. Kunhikannan, the entomologist of the Mysore Government, from whose book I have already quoted, gives a true picture of many British cold-weather visitors to India as follows:—

"The English traveller, who hurries through the cities of British India and the capitals of the princes, still regards India as a land of wealth and magnificence; yet had the same traveller included a village in his itinerary and looked at the faces gathered round him, most of them hungry, emaciated, and with torn clothing, meek and humble beyond words, he would have found that there was starvation, distress, and disease on a scale such as he had never associated with any other country in the world. But what does he care for the humanity of India? He came out to see the Taj, the sunset on the Himalayas, to meet the European merchant princes and Indian princes, to visit Kalighat, and to declare to his own circle of admiring friends that he had 'seen India,' and so the myth of India's fabulous wealth survives."

Yet in reality India—along with China, which is almost on the same level—is by all reckoning the poorest country in the world; and the most serious and alarming fact of all is this: that in both countries the poverty to-day appears to be increasing.

For a trained observer who wishes to investigate thoroughly, a long residence in remote country districts, outside the areas of the large towns, is essential. This would have to be carried out, not with the paraphernalia of a foreigner or a high Government official, but with something of the simplicity of the villagers themselves. Only by thus settling down in close contact with the village people is it possible patiently to learn their troubles and to obtain a real understanding of their sufferings and wants.

Many of the stark, statistical facts of Indian poverty collected from unimpeachable sources have been given in Lala Lajpat Rai's remarkable book called *Unhappy India*. The author was one of my greatest friends, a man of the people, devoted to his own villagers in the Punjab, and at all times ready to suffer with them and for them. Very few people in the north of India knew the needs of the poor people as well as he did: and yet the Punjab is by no means the poorest part of India. After he had attained phenomenal success at the Bar as the leading lawyer of his province, his whole fortune was spent in relief of the poor. He was himself born in a poor village as a member of a very poor family. Therefore he loved the poor with all his heart, and founded before he died "The Servants of the People Society," whose object is to undertake new ventures on their behalf and investigate the economic causes underlying their poverty. Some of the noblest men in India have become life members of this society, giving up their whole time to its work.

In *Unhappy India* he takes different periods in the last sixty years, and shows by unimpeachable evidence how chronic the state of India's impoverishment has become.

One of the first of the writers whom he quotes is Sir William Hunter, the great historian of Orissa and also of India generally, who was appointed Director of Statistics in the 'seventies of last century. He puts on record a statement, which has since been often quoted, that in British India alone, omitting the Indian States, forty million people lived and died in a state of such abject misery that hardly ever were they able to satisfy their hunger. They passed through life in a state of permanent suffering owing to lack of food, thus painfully enduring a half-starved and emaciated existence.

This figure of forty millions has never been challenged, and yet it meant at the time nearly one-fifth of the population of British India. Since, in the last seventy years, this population has nearly doubled, the figure which Sir William Hunter quoted might now be largely increased. Such statistics as these are staggering; the human mind reels under them, especially when one comes to think of *individuals*—of women and little children as well as men. Yet when famine conditions are declared in any province, owing to the failure of the monsoon, these normal miseries which are already almost intolerable become inconceivably worse. Only those who have had personal experience of famine conditions, in what is called a "famine area," can realize the long-drawn agony of human existence in those circumstances. Furthermore, in India the losses caused by floods over vast areas, when disease follows close upon the draining away of the surface waters, are hardly less acute.

Sir George Grierson is Lala Lajpat Rai's second authority. He also was a great statistician under the Government of India, and he possessed an intimate knowledge of Indian village life. His reputation in his own generation was as high as that of Sir William Hunter's had been twenty years earlier.

"Briefly," he writes, "all persons in India of the labouring class and 10 per cent of the artisan or cultivating classes, or 45 per cent of the total population, are insufficiently fed, or housed, or both. It follows that nearly one hundred millions of people in British India are living in extreme poverty."

Here again the figures to-day must be largely increased, not only because of the growth of population, but also because the poverty itself has become more widespread in recent years.

Coming down to later times, Mr. Manohar Lal, who has been many times an executive member of the Punjab Government and has also won a name both at Cambridge and in India as an economic expert, writes as follows:—

"Poverty, grinding poverty, is a tremendous fact of our economic and national position: and it is to my mind an immeasurably more potent fact than even the ignorance and illiteracy that prevails among the masses. It is a picture of literal starvation, mental and physical. It can represent the life of no unit of civilized humanity."

These words were written in 1916, during the years that were comparatively prosperous; for India, at the beginning of the European War, received considerable benefit from the rise in world prices, especially cotton and jute.

Coming down later still, to a period after the war, when for a few years another wave of high prices swept over America and Europe, Dr. H. H. Mann, Director of Agriculture in Bombay, gave the following statement to the *Times of India*:

"Although the standard of living of the agriculturists has undoubtedly improved, I could not say that the majority of the people are living up to that standard. My enquiries have shown me, in fact, that fully 75 per cent of the people in the 'famine tracts' are living so much below their own standard that their economic position has to be reckoned as unsound, whilst even in the areas which are looked upon as reasonably prosperous there are only 66 per cent of the people in a sound economic position."

Dr. Mann admitted that it was most difficult to make any detailed observations on this point because there were so few reliable data, but his candid opinion, after twenty years' careful investigation, was this: that while in those two decades the standard of life in the villages had improved, the actual relationship of the bulk of the people towards that standard had not improved in a similar manner.

Dr. Mann went further, and explained that little could be done on any extensive scale until the Government and the social reformers both recognized that the secret of the whole prosperity of the agricultural population was the filling of their stomachs. The empty stomach was the greatest obstacle to progress in India, and he wished to emphasize that all efforts should ultimately concentrate on filling the stomachs of the people.

When asked what measures he would suggest for this great work of filling the empty stomachs of the masses, Dr. Mann said that much could be done by the people themselves. They must put themselves to work. No country could ever hope to be prosperous if the majority of its population remained idle for six months in the year. The people must be given some work, no matter how small the income derived therefrom, during the dry season. No matter in what other way Mr. Gandhi might have gone astray, he had penetrated into the secret of the poverty of India when he advocated the spinning-wheel, even if it did produce only a few annas a day. He therefore thought that the Government should pay the closest attention to this "village industry" phase of the problem, if they ever hoped to have a prosperous countryside. He expressed bewilderment that so long a period had elapsed before the Government had tackled this village industrial problem in right earnest.

Dr. Mann's last message to the people of India was that he had the greatest hopes of the Bombay Presidency reaching a very high standard of economic prosperity, wherein the villagers themselves would participate. But no endeavour towards such a better state of things could be made by a people with empty stomachs. So his last message to the people of the land, to all social workers, and to those in charge of the administration, was that they should devise means whereby the cultivators might be given sufficient food.

In his investigations he had taken a typical village named Pimpla, and made a very exhaustive enquiry. He had then compared this with other villages, and had found that his average was correct. In the concluding chapter of his Report he writes: "Out of 103 families investigated, 35 per cent can pay their way in the standard they themselves lay down. The others are living below that standard, and this conclusion, which seems very clear, forms an exceedingly serious state of affairs."

If Dr. Mann had been writing in the year 1937 instead of 1927, he would have drawn a much darker picture; for the strain of the years 1930–5, when the raw products of agriculture reached their lowest marketable limit and the trade balance of India was only kept up by huge exports of gold from the country, increased the indebtedness of the Indian peasant as much as fourfold in some provinces, and every effort had to be made by the provincial legislatures to scale down the debts in order to save the country-side from utter ruin. Since the year 1935 a slight improvement has been registered, and the monsoon rains, on which everything depends, have been fairly good over a series of years. But the war in the Far East has once more dislocated trade in an abnormal manner, and some of the staple crops such as cotton have suffered very heavily. Since India has now come definitely into the world market these vast fluctuations in prices, owing to the unsettled state of world affairs, affect Indian trade as much as that of other countries.

It may here be repeated with emphasis that such conditions of penurious living among vast multitudes of the Indian population do not in any way lend themselves to sexual excess, such as the authors who have written sensationally about India have placarded before the public. For such bare, stark poverty is hardly compatible with extravagance of that kind. This simple fact must continually be borne in mind when dealing with India to-day.

There was indeed a certain period in the remote past—at a time when the population of India was small and the soil very rich and fertile—that *did* appear to lend itself to these excesses, which are the product of luxury rather than want. This may be one of the causes of the frankly obscene sculpture which still disgraces the outer walls of many Hindu temples. But this period was not a long one, as far as the monuments record it; nor does it appear in any way to have been universal in India. It is a significant fact that these carvings attract very little attention to-day. They pass almost unnoticed.

If it be asked whether this extreme poverty of India is always to remain in the same unrelieved and unrelievable state, the answer is surely in the negative. The national awakening itself (as I have shown) is sweeping away abuses, and the villages of India have now felt the power of that great impulse hardly less than the towns. Hinduism itself is stripping off many of its old outworn customs, which have seriously impeded scientific progress in the past both in agriculture and in social living. Above all, there are thousands of national workers in every province who are building up a fresh economic structure which will give profitable work to the villagers.

"The bulk of the population," writes Mr. Gandhi, "is agricultural, and Indian agriculture involves very hard work for certain short periods and almost complete inactivity for the rest of the year. These periods of inactivity are, in the great majority of cases, spent in idleness. But where the cultivator pursues some craft which will employ him and his family at times when they are not required in the fields—a craft in which continuity of employment is not essential—the proceeds of that craft are a saving from waste and therefore a clear gain. The most typical of such crafts and the one most widely pursued is the production of homespun cotton cloth for daily use."

Thus the new economy, which is being slowly built up by the earnest endeavours of those who see in these village industries the salvation of their own country, may in time restore a margin of relief from utter penury. It will not be necessary to use the ruthless pressure of centralized industries to drive the rural population into the towns. This new village economy contemplates the industrialization of the village life itself. If, owing to the remarkable enthusiasm which has been generated by the national movement, this can be accomplished, the grave moral evils of the town life will be avoided, and the open-air life of the country will be still preserved for the vast majority of the Indian population.

The possibilities of this combination of agriculture and industry have already been tried out with success in countries like Denmark and Switzerland. In Ireland also there has been a village reconstruction attempted of the same character. The extraordinary thrift of the Indian peasant should form a good foundation for the Indian experiment.

These village industries are immediately practicable, because: (1) They do not require costly implements or large capital investment. (2) They need only very moderate skill such as the poverty-stricken masses of India can easily acquire. (3) They can be undertaken by women as well as men, and by the aged as well as the young. (4) The tradition of village industries is still alive in the country, and only needs revival. (5) The yarn produced by spinning can be used at once for domestic purposes, and the surplus can be sold in markets which are close at hand. (6) They can be carried on at times of flood and famine when agriculture itself has become impossible, and thus are an insurance against a bad monsoon.

Therefore, in the near future, though India may never even wish to reach at any stage of its progress the income per head of the Western nations, its standard may still be raised (as self-government increases) above its present level. Its aim will never be to surpass other powers in luxurious living: it will rather aim at that simplicity which is compatible with a high moral standard and a true spiritual growth.

Chapter 14

THE PROBLEM OF POPULATION

Of all the vitally important questions affecting the social and moral life of modern India, that of over-population has received up to the present time the least thorough investigation and enquiry. Its effect on Indian character has been ignored by the sensational writers who seek to draw lurid pictures of India's moral decline.

The more one studies the problem, the more this overcrowding is seen to be at the root of India's poverty, want, and unemployment. It also accounts for that malnutrition which makes any sustained effort difficult. Furthermore, it is now a burning question, which presses every year more and more urgently for a solution as it reaches alarming proportions. While Soviet Russia shows a parallel increase, there are still in Siberia vast tracts of country crying out for a larger population. But in India the agricultural land has already been occupied almost up to the margin of profitable cultivation.

It has been estimated by the Census Commissioners, and the Viceroy has publicly stated, that unless some major disaster occurs (such as a vast epidemic or a famine on a large scale) the population is likely to exceed four hundred millions by the year 1941, when the next census is to be taken. Such figures are enormous, and it is difficult for the human mind to take them in with any realization of their significance. They imply that about eighty million more human beings will have been added to India's population between 1921 and 1941. All these will have become a further burden on an already crowded soil, making the units of cultivation, which have already reached an unproductive level, still smaller. To compare this with Europe, it means that a population as large as that of modern Germany will have been added to India in twenty years.

Not even China, with all its dense masses of human life, has ever shown such an immense increase in so short a time. No new irrigation schemes, such as the Sukkur barrage, and no new scientific methods of agriculture and animal husbandry can do much to ease the pressure of entirely new population on so large a scale. The round of birth and death goes on amid suffering hard to picture or describe.

There are increasingly few possibilities now of any further migration to countries near at hand or from one province to another. In earlier days these outlets drew off some millions of India's rapid growth, but the saturation point among these neighbours has nearly been reached. In Burma, which is still not sufficiently developed, Indians have become unwelcome because of their superior thrift, and the same is beginning to be true about Ceylon. Only in Assam is there still not only vacant land, but also a demand in the tea plantations for more agricultural labour. Yet the numbers that can be absorbed year by year is comparatively small, and if for any cause this number is too rapidly expanded a fresh disaster may occur such as the "Chandpur" incident of 1921, when the tea-garden labourers left the gardens for want of proper employment.

To go farther afield, Malaya cannot take a bigger quota from the south of India than it does at present. Rubber restriction is likely to continue and make a larger labour supply not needed from Madras Presidency. The British colonies, which had absorbed a certain amount of Indian indentured labour in times now gone by, have no desire to take any more Indian immigrants since indenture has been abolished. Natal is even seeking, by a system of bonus and free passages, to repatriate some of those who had already become domiciled; and there is no more pitiable problem to-day than that of the returned emigrants who cluster round the docks of Calcutta and Madras seeking to obtain a passage back to the colonies where many of them were born.

East Africa has been recently pointed out as a possible new ground for Indian immigration on a large scale. But those who have studied the question thoroughly and know the conditions are aware that the number which could be provided for along that coast would necessarily be very small. They would hardly be noticeable when the increase in India now runs to over three millions every year and is likely to reach four millions very soon. When the South African Government sought to discover a country where some new colonization scheme might serve to attract Indians from Natal, the results of the investigation were almost entirely negative, even though the Union Government for political reasons was ready to spend large sums of money in making it a success. The question of Brazil was carefully considered, but the unsettled government of that country made emigration very difficult. Borneo was the only country recommended for further enquiry, and the results of the investigation were not encouraging.

The causes of this exceedingly rapid increase of population in India are many in number. The monsoon rains during the past twenty years have been fairly regular. Hitherto there has been no complete failure causing famine: on the contrary, there have been local floods which have brought with them disasters of a minor character. The peace of this large sub-continent, which India represents, has been practically unbroken. There have been no wars to be compared with that which is now being carried on in the Far East or the Great War in Europe.

The joint family system, in spite of its many virtues, has one very serious and almost fatal drawback at such a time of crisis as India is now passing through. It sets a premium on early marriage, because the newly married couple do not have to find a home for themselves, but are accommodated within the larger family circle. This arrangement may be admirable when further population is badly needed, but it is most harmful at a time when everything should be done to delay the age of marriage, and so produce fewer but physically stronger children.

Though it is true, as has already been pointed out, that the age of marriage in India is being slowly raised and acts of legislation have ratified the process, nevertheless there are no clear signs as yet that the fecundity of the marriages which now take place is in any way diminishing. The population figures themselves show this. Therefore the pressure on the soil of these added millions of human lives can only end in poverty and unemployment becoming even greater than it ever was before. There seems no escape from this vicious circle of added misery.

The saddest fact of all has yet to be mentioned. For along with this enormous increase in population year by year the average, normal expectation of each human life has been decreasing to a terribly low figure. While in Great Britain and Norway and Sweden the average length of human life is continually increasing and now stands between fifty and sixty, and in New Zealand has surpassed even sixty years in duration, in India it is still below twenty-five, and the average span of life is actually diminishing. This implies that men and women are cut off from being a profit to the community by an early death just at the time when their skill and ability would have been of the greatest possible value. The whole of India has mourned the loss of outstanding men such as G. K. Gokhale and C. R. Das and others whose intellectual eminence and devotion to their country could ill be spared. Yet the number of such men and women of the highest character who die young still goes on increasing. It is not merely climate or disease which causes this, but lack of stamina and vitality.

Recently the staff at the Pasteur Institute at Coonoor has been working out on scientific lines, by means of careful experiment, the problem of malnutrition, the effects of which are visible over large areas of India. The results of their investigations have now been very widely published, and Mahatma Gandhi has taken the deepest interest in them, realizing their vast importance. What they have found to be true has corroborated the earlier statements made by the most reliable statisticians in the past whose figures I have quoted. They show that a very large percentage of the population of India is under-nourished, and that a considerable proportion is living below the level of subsistence. Only the warmth and light of the Indian sun, saturating the human body day after day, makes this at all possible.

Even the rice, which is by far the commonest food of the Indian people, has lost much of its nutritive value since the milling processes by machinery have been introduced. In earlier days, when it was milled by hand, the outer skin wherein lies the best nourishment of all was kept intact. Now it is polished away by machinery, and though hand-milling still goes on, the insidious cheapness of the machine process wins its own way, and the hand-milling, which is tedious and irksome, is abandoned. Just the same thing has happened which took place when the cheap cotton goods of Lancashire superseded the hand-made village cloth. Mahatma Gandhi, more than any other person, by an almost superhuman effort is endeavouring to restore these valuable hand processes which give employment in the villages during the dry, hot season of the year when ploughing has become impossible.

Here the whole question of industrialization has to be faced as a means of absorbing the surplus population and adding to the wealth of India. At first sight there seems to be here an attractive solution of both problems—both poverty and overpopulation. But the more the whole question is studied on the spot, the less adequate such a short cut seems. For where already this industrialization has taken place it has led to a new crop of evils that are worse in some ways than penury itself. What happened in England at the time of the industrial revolution has been happening on a large scale in India to-day.

But it may be suggested that strict factory legislation and what is called the nationalization of industries might remove those evils, and thus make the migration of the village surplus population to the towns and then back to the villages comparatively innocuous. While these social efforts might improve matters, they do not seem to me in any way to provide an adequate solution of India's double problem. For the scope for central factories, run on Western lines and on the gigantic scale which we are used to in America and Europe, appears to be entirely out of keeping with the rural economy of India. Her mineral wealth and hydro-electric power are now fairly well known, and they have none of those vast and almost illimitable supplies which we associate with the United States and Soviet Russia and the continent of Europe. Furthermore the climate of India, which lies for a great part of its surface in the tropics, is entirely unsuitable for huge centralized industries such as are carried on in the colder climates of the world to-day. India, as a country, must and will always remain predominantly agricultural. Its assets are not oil and coal and minerals, but brilliant sunshine and copious monsoon rains and alluvial soils.

The natural process, therefore, of India's industrial development does not consist in driving the surplus village population into the already overcrowded cities, but rather in giving them opportunities of developing arts and crafts in the villages themselves, filling up their spare time when agriculture is impossible with industries that can be intermittent. Hydro-electric power should not be concentrated in town areas, but distributed over the numberless villages. He who can solve the problem of the transmission of electric power without leakage will have done much also to solve the twin problems of poverty and over-population in India. But that solution may still be far distant, and meanwhile the problem itself become more intricate. The time factor is all the while working against us.

Remedies which lie close at hand may now be

considered. While they offer no immediate solution of the problem, they do appear to give a gleam of hope for the future and can be undertaken immediately.

The first is the rapid spread of education among the girls as well as boys, which shall reach the villages as well as the towns. For if education becomes a national enthusiasm, as it has already become in Soviet Russia, it will accustom the parents to the thought of postponing the marriage age of their sons and daughters. Customs which are altogether evil, such as child marriage, can only be done away with completely and finally by the vigorous growth of public opinion. Legislation is only valuable in registering that growth: for no reform is safe that depends on legislation alone and has not got the general consent of public opinion behind it. Laws become a dead letter if they have not the moral conscience of men and women to support them.

One great advantage, that has only recently accrued, has been the handing over of responsible government in the provinces to the people and their representatives. For where religious tradition is concerned the people must act on their own initiative. No foreigner, however sympathetic, can now pass laws which change the customs of religion among the common people. Lord Bentinck could do this a hundred years ago when the popular mind was apathetic. He could abolish *Sati* with the stroke of a pen. But the British rulers as the century advanced became more cautious. They waited quite rightly for public opinion to be formed behind them before they dared to take action. Yet where the legislation is passed by those who belong to the same country and the same religion there is much more chance of its ordinances being respected. Thus to-day the national awakening which has led on to responsible government is already having its beneficial effect. For the idea is gaining ground even in remote villages that child marriages are harmful to the nation, and that Mahatma Gandhi has set his face sternly against them. When Congress Ministers in office carry out his mandate, the whole country will accept the new law and act upon it.

As an added power, the women of India themselves every year are taking a far more active and intelligent part in national affairs. The extraordinary growth of this gracious influence, even during the past few years, must give us hope. For when the women of India make up their minds that a thing ought to be done, there is a power of devotion, goodness, and sacrifice behind them which is invincible. I have already mentioned the value of girls' education carried on to a much higher standard, which can by its very presence create an idea in people's minds incompatible with child marriage. It is here that the women who have taken up with enthusiasm and devotion the national cause can help best of all; for they can speak to their own fellow women as no men can, and they will be heard. The value of this is no mere guesswork, because it has already led to practical results. In the colonies, where Indians have gone abroad to do the same agricultural work and live the same village life which they live in India, it has been found out by direct experience that wherever girls' education has been increased and the parents have learnt to see its advantage, the age at which girls are married automatically advances. It is all within the scope of women's work, and under the new national impulse great improvements may be expected.

Along with wider education and the national awakening of womanhood must go religious revival in a country so wedded to religion as India. For a new religious sanction is needed and a new religious tradition must be built up. This has already been accomplished on the part of the reforming religious movements. Among the Sikhs and Parsees and Indian Christians, as also among the members of the Arya Samaj and the Brahma Samaj and other similar bodies, the religious motive itself has been used to advance the cause of marriage on healthier and better lines. If orthodox Hinduism were to give way on this point under the pressure of all these religious reform movements, the result might be very great indeed.

What may be rightly affirmed is this: that the devolution of responsibility upon Indians themselves has come at the right moment. It must be carried forward with all speed if the highly critical situation due to poverty and over-population is to be met in time. For only as the whole mind and will of the people are bent upon overcoming these new difficulties will there by any possibility of success. Rulers coming from outside, however benevolent, can never be expected to achieve what popular democratic rule can accomplish. On the tide of the national movement much may be done. Many social abuses, such as untouchability and child marriage, may be swept away and the simple village people of India may become healthy and thriving once more.

It will be noticed in all that I have written that I have not mentioned hitherto the "short cut" of birth control and contraception. Apart from the fact that Mahatma Gandhi has already condemned it in quite unmeasured terms and that it does extreme violence to all Hindu sentiment, the solution that it offers can hardly be regarded as having any immediate importance. For in the vast majority of the Indian villages, as things are at present, such a remedy has not the remotest chance of coming either within the means or the inclination of at least 99 per cent of the Indian village people. For these and other reasons it is not a practical proposition on any large scale to-day, and we are bound to seek for remedies elsewhere. The greatest remedy of all I find in the national movement itself and in the wonderful power of Mahatma Gandhi, through its means, to bring about desperately needed reforms.

Chapter 15

KALIGHAT

Miss Mayo's description of the slaughter of goats at Kalighat, Calcutta, and her chapter about cruelties practised on dumb animals, both deserve very serious consideration. For such cruelties as she has described do still take place; and wherever they exist they are a standing disgrace. It is not possible to offer any defence for them at all; for cruelty to dumb animals is evil all the world over, and it is terribly prevalent in some unspeakable forms in India.

It is, however, necessary to point out that she has said nothing at all about the other side of the picture. For while it is true that in certain temples animal sacrifices are still offered, it is also true that Hinduism in the great majority of its places of worship has abandoned animal sacrifice altogether, and substituted for it the beautiful custom of offering flowers. This is by far the most usual form of worship in India to-day. It owes its origin to the tender precepts of the Buddhist and Jain faiths, and also to the Vaishnava cult which sprang up along with them and in the end superseded them. In a thousand ways this gentle compassion towards animal life has now become a daily practice, so that, with many millions of devout Hindus, the slaughter of any animal, either for food or worship, is a thing utterly abhorrent.

With regard to the relics of animal sacrifice, such as the scene at Kalighat, no drama of modern times has ever been written which is more tremendous in its denunciation of Kalighat, and all that it stands for, than the play called *Visarjan* (in English, "Sacrifice"), written by Rabindranath Tagore. It is acted openly in Calcutta, close to Kalighat itself. It has also been placed on the films, where its plain lesson has appealed far more widely than on the stage itself.

This play has always been one of the most popular among the poet's dramas, and it attracts large audiences who deeply appreciate its moral bearing. He himself has taken part in it, and has trained his own students as actors. In every way possible, both by his own deeds and writings, he has stood out against this monstrous evil of Kalighat. Such open denunciation would have been impossible in Calcutta itself without causing a riot, if there were any religious vitality left in these hateful practices of animal sacrifice. They are clearly moribund, catering merely for the ignorant and superstitious among the lowest ranks of the huge population which is gathered in the metropolis.

It is indeed altogether inexcusable that a united storm of protest from the whole educated community has not already been raised long ago against this horrible custom, such as would have brought it to a speedy end. There is clearly a moral weakness in allowing these cruelties to go lingering on when the whole attitude of educated society is against them.

But this weakness runs through India, and has to be taken into account at every turn by every true moral reformer. We have to probe down very deep and find out its ultimate causes. For it is probably true to-day that India is the one highly civilized and humane country where the slaughter of animals as an act of worship *to appease the angry gods* is still openly practised by ignorant people and connived at by the enlightened. It is one of these debasing anachronisms which reveals a lack of moral fibre in those who are leaders of public opinion.

Yet is there not a beam in our own eye in the West? Is it nothing that the killing of dumb animals for human food has ceased altogether among Hindus over a great part of India while it is being daily practised among ourselves? Is it nothing that the slaughter-houses, where these dumb animals would be driven, are rarely seen in India, while they are a commonplace with ourselves? No country in the world can show a higher or nobler record in this direction than Hindu India.

It was the pure moral instinct of pity which was able to accomplish such a startling change as the abstinence from meat-eating in a people numbering many millions. A religion which could thus restrain the brute appetite of man, for the sake of the animals for whom man had compassion, cannot possibly in its essence be cruel. Its humane power is still active in modern life, and as a living creed to-day it carries those who profess it much further in their mercy towards the animal creation than the West is yet prepared to go.

To come back to the specific charges which have often been made—there are cruelties practised by ignorant drivers on draught animals which are quite as inexcusable as the religious slaughter at Kalighat. There are practices with regard to the extraction of the last drop of milk from cows, by the practice of *Phooka*, which are abominably cruel. There is also more rarely practised the flaying alive of goats, which is hideously brutal. All these are just as fiendish and devilish as those commercial practices of the West by which animal life is taken in an equally abominable manner for greed of gain. No one can read without shame concerning the method by which wild animals are trapped in the West merely in order to provide expensive furs for luxurious women. Everything should be done by every humane man or woman of whatever race to abolish these things from off the earth immediately, and in this direction every help is needed.

These cruelties, as I have tried to show, are not typical of India, any more than Kalighat is typical of the Hindu religion. They are horrible and unspeakable aberrations, not the normal practice.

Rather it is typical of Hindu India, and of no other religious country in the world, that the smaller animals, especially the birds and squirrels, have entirely forgotten their fear of the human race, together with all the never-ending torture that this fear involves. In the avenues and gardens, and even along the open streets, these timid creatures have become so completely free from alarm that they will flutter and scramble about near to one's feet, or around one's head, in complete confidence of the kindly nature of man. Only this morning, on the day I am writing this chapter, a squirrel began to play all round about me as I sat in the veranda, and even scrambled over my feet, without a shadow of fear; and again, while I went out walking in the early morning, the birds sang on quite undisturbed by my presence. They hopped about close to my feet, and also went on with their songs while I passed under the trees. Such a harmony between man and nature has taken centuries to knit together. It is one of the most beautiful things in the world which has to be seen to be understood. What peace and freedom and joy this absence of all trace of fear denotes to millions of tiny, fluttering creatures can more easily be imagined than described.

The Hindu religion has actually brought this into practice by enunciating the principle of *Ahimsa*, or freedom from violence. The creed is fulfilled in action. It would not be easy to name a parallel humane conquest, in the annals of mankind, which has touched animal life. If, therefore, on certain other sides evil habits of cruelty still hold sway in India, the victory over them cannot be long delayed, because the conscience of the Hindu people is already won over.

The West, on its side, hardly yet realizes how deeply and sincerely the educated people in India respect the Society for the Prevention of Cruelty to Animals; or again the kindred New Health Movement, which works towards a more complete vegetarian diet, together with other similar humane institutions. At the same time they regard with horror such facts as the shambles of Chicago; they find utterly unreadable such a book as Upton Sinclair's *Jungle*, with its description of the slaughter-houses; they are intensely shocked by the narratives and pictures of the Western blood sports, undertaken solely for amusement. The hunting down to the death of panic-stricken deer by dogs and men; the shooting of hundreds of birds in a single day, with all the torture of the wounded that are not killed outright; the chasing of terrorized wild animals by a pack of hounds ravenous for blood—these and other so-called amusements create a horror in the mind of a Buddhist, or a Jain, or Vaishnava devotee. The question also of the vivisection of animals is not an open one in India. The practice is abhorred.

I have watched the most striking instances of wild animals living in harmony with mankind at different times when I have been with Hindu ascetics, who live day and night, where wild beasts and snakes abound, entirely unprotected and entirely unharmed. I can remember seeing a whole colony of wild monkeys seated gravely round one such ascetic—an old man with a long white beard—as he gave them food and talked to them, keeping them in order with a nod. The boy who was with him told me that every day the old man would come to that particular spot and hold the same gathering, and then go back to his meditation. At Brindaban, near to Muttra, the woods and groves and river banks have very many recluses who have thus become friends of the whole animal world. In the personal memoir I have written concerning Sadhu Sundar Singh similar instances have been told.[1]

After long residence in India it was repulsive to me, on landing at Marseilles, to see a large butcher's shop in a public square where meat was exposed. It had meant nothing to me before; and as a lad I had passed such shops day after day without a single thought of the suffering which they implied. But my stay in the heart of India had altered the whole perspective. When I have mentioned this incident to Hindu friends, they have told me that this was one of the first shocks which they met in the West. Such shops could easily be avoided in India, as they were comparatively few; but they seemed to be everywhere in Western towns, and they always created a revulsion of feeling with regard to the slaughter of animal life which they denoted.

While therefore we rightly condemn, along with most Indians themselves, the revolting practices at Kalighat and the gross cruelties to animals in the Calcutta streets, it is surely unfair when giving an account of the treatment of animals in India to pass over those things that the poet Wordsworth has

[1] See *Sadhu Sundar Singh: A Personal Memoir*, published by Hodder and Stoughton, London, p. 164.

called "the little unremembered acts of kindness and of love" which are prevalent everywhere in India and help to make up so large a portion of a good man's life.

One further question remains which has to be faced before the whole problem of cruelty to animals (as a Hindu faces it) can be solved. It centres in the actual taking of life of man or beast. The pure disciple of *Ahimsa* is a pacifist to the very core of his being, and he has learnt to go much further than the pacifism of the West. He would hate to take the life of an animal just as much as he would hate to take the life of a human being.

This is an abstract doctrine carrying with it the sheer logic that appeals strongly to the Hindu mind: but it is difficult to put it completely into practice. It is a common sight, for instance, to see the Jain ascetic with a piece of white cloth before his mouth so that the tiniest midge may not enter it as he breathes: but those who study micro-organisms know how much further life can be found than those insects which can be seen with the naked eye. Yet there is a nobility about this ideal which cannot be gainsaid. Newman's famous definition of a gentleman, as one who never inflicts pain, comes near to it from a different angle. Nevertheless, in hard, concrete, everyday life it is being found more and more impossible to put it into practice.

Once upon a time the Vaishnava Community in Bengal made a representation to me at Santiniketan that I would intervene in order to persuade the

Government of India to prohibit all shooting of wild animals within the *Chauassi Kōs* (eighty-four square miles) at Brindaban, which was peculiarly sacred in their religion. I very gladly took up this cause, but was immediately faced with the difficulties of the cultivators whose crops would be destroyed by the depredations of wild animals if no drastic action against them could be taken.

The first instinct of an Englishman when he sees an animal in agonizing suffering is to put it out of its misery. Mahatma Gandhi, in his Asram at Sabarmati, did this to a calf that lingered on for days without any possibility of cure. He gave it an injection, and its suffering was peacefully ended. But in Hindu India only a Mahatma could do such a thing with impunity and without feeling it to be a sin. For this reason half-starved, decrepit cattle are constantly met with, whose existence is nothing less than a prolonged drawn-out pain. Even more wretched still sometimes are the pariah dogs.

It is not cruelty which is at the back of this, though the sight of such miserable and decrepit animals is apt to produce mere callousness in lapse of time. What it really proceeds from is an intense belief in the sanctity of all life. That belief, in itself, is surely worthy of respect. It does not deserve to be condemned without a single thought. What is much more urgently required is this: that we in the West should not pass harsh judgments on Hindus and their religious instincts, but rather seek to understand.

It has been of profound interest to me to find that my dear friend, Dr. Albert Schweitzer of Lambarene, in Central Africa, while seeking for a philosophy which shall lead humanity forward in the modern age, has hit upon this very phrase, "the sanctity of all life," or (as he puts it in another place) "reverence for life." This is a motto which has been current in India for more than two thousand years. If I understand him rightly, however, he would himself take life when it seemed the lesser of two evils and if the superior necessity compelled him; but, like Gandhi, he would act with regret, realizing that the main principle of his own line of action was being discarded.

Perhaps there is a point somewhere betwixt and between, where the Englishman's carelessness about the slaughter of animals and the Hindu's scrupulous carefulness to avoid such destruction of life may meet. Possibly Dr. Albert Schweitzer, in the last volume of his philosophy, called *Civilization and Ethics*, may tell us where the line may be drawn. Up to the present no theory leading to a harmony between philosophy and ethics on this subject has been formulated which satisfies both reason and conscience among the different peoples of mankind. The one thing therefore needed from either side is to avoid bringing railing accusations, which indict whole nations as cruel and inhuman.

Thoughts such as these lead on to the consideration of Hinduism as a religion which is extremely difficult for the West to understand. Certain aspects where such difficulties occur will be dealt with in the next chapter. In making this attempt to explain I am aware that I am only touching the fringe of a vast subject, but this will be better than refraining from making any attempt at all.

Chapter 16

HINDUISM AS A RELIGION

THERE are certain things that make Hinduism, as a living religion, very difficult for the West to understand—especially for those who are members of reformed Churches and live in the colder northern climate, where nature is stern and hard rather than full of colour and warmth and brightness. It is so easy to be offended by these surface things, which are repellent, and to take no account of the deep inner spirit that lies beneath.

This was the initial mistake of the older Protestant missionaries who came to India in the early nineteenth century. They had a genuine hatred of all forms of idol worship and were apt to regard Hinduism, on account of certain indefensible practices, as altogether vicious and immoral. Their own sombre theology, based largely on certain portions of the Old Testament, aided and abetted such one-sided opinions.[1]

Before these earlier missionaries, however, had determined thus to condemn Hinduism (just at a time when it was reforming itself from within) they should have learnt humbly from Church history that the Christian religion itself had gone through its periods of decline, during which it also became incredibly corrupt. If any foreigner had noted the

[1] See Introduction, p. 14.

external aspects of Christendom during such times of decay as the Dark Ages, or just before the Reformation, he might have pointed out the evils that then appeared to be inherent in the Christian faith itself. But we all know that such a judgment would have been both short-sighted and unjust. For at the end of each period of decline there has been a marvellous revival.

In the same manner to-day there has been a revival in Hinduism, which has proceeded from within and has very rapidly transformed its structure. Men and women in large numbers have not only given up all in the cause of religion, in order to spend their lives in quiet meditation seeking God's presence, but they also have led the way forward to reforms which have changed the lives of millions of people. There has been, in every part of India, a clearing away of old abuses and a setting up of new moral standards. This has proved, if proof were needed, that there is a deep spring of spiritual energy ready to burst forth, with cleansing and purifying streams, as soon as ever the debris accumulated in the past has been removed.

Probably the older forms of the Christian religion, such as are observed in the Roman and Greek Churches, have more points in common with very conservative Eastern religions, like Hinduism and Buddhism, than the bare external features of the Protestant Churches of northern Europe. There is a natural love of ceremony in southern Europe, as there is also in all tropical countries. This is often combined with a readiness to allow the ancient animistic cults to find their setting under new names within the higher religion.

We can see this carried to its farthest limits in the forms of the Christian religion which are to-day professed in Central and South America. We also have similar features in what have been called the unreformed Churches of Abyssinia and Egypt.

Those of us who have been nurtured from childhood in the reformed faith are too apt to pass harsh judgment on these older conservative forms of the Christian religion. We have sometimes wished to abolish them altogether; for they seem to be contrary to our ideas of a truly spiritual faith. I can vividly remember the shock which Principal S. K. Rudra of St. Stephen's College, Delhi, received when he went for the first time into a Coptic Church at Port Said while our steamer was in port. He came out horrified and said to me, "Why, the inside of that church, with its images and candles, is just like a Hindu or Buddhist temple. It is not my idea of a Christian church at all!"

He had been brought up for the most part in a puritan tradition, and these externals of worship shocked him as much as they would have shocked a pious Musalman.

The earlier missionaries who went out from the northern countries of Europe and America were shocked in the same manner. With their puritan zeal, they earnestly endeavoured to set up a new reformed worship in place of the ancient ceremonial which had survived for so many centuries. Thus there are now reformed Protestant congregations in Egypt and Abyssinia, Travancore and Malabar, whose members have been won over by missionary propaganda from the old orthodox Churches. Yet even in the Protestant North of Europe and America this process of destroying that which has survived for so many centuries is now being openly questioned. It is commonly agreed that the process has been carried too far, and that a gradual reform from within these orthodox Churches may be more in accord with the general principles of Christian teaching such as we find in the Sermon on the Mount. The "Golden Rule"—to do to others as we would wish them to do to us—has been seen to apply in these cases. Ruthless iconoclasm is clearly out of harmony with the main tenor of Christ's teaching. "Let both grow together," He said, "until the harvest."

This fact, with regard to our own Christian religion, should make us more charitable also towards certain unreformed types of Hinduism. For there are serious dangers always underlying this reforming process from which Christendom has by no means escaped unharmed—as modern Germany appears to be showing us to-day. The parable of the tares and the wheat has its own very striking place in Christ's teaching, and ardent reformers of abuses have been apt to disregard it.

In mentioning these things, I am simply putting forward the plea for a more careful and considerate judgment than many modern writers from the West have formed of Hinduism on very short acquaintance. I do not for a moment desire to condone things that are still being practised, such as the *devadasi* system,[1] or untouchability, or animal slaughter as a form of religious worship, which ought long ago to have been swept away. I admire very greatly the noble work that has been done by the Brahma Samaj, the Arya Samaj, and other reforming movements. Also I would gladly recognize the deep religious fervour, combined with devotion to works of mercy and charity, which characterizes the Ramakrishna Mission.

My own ardent Christian faith is well known, and I long to share the joy of it with others. At the same time, in Christ's own teaching and in that of St. Paul I find it repeatedly written that the true Christian must pay tender regard to all that is pure and noble and lovely and of good report, wherever it may be found, so that the God of peace may be with him (Phil. iv. 8, 9). It is in the light of this teaching from my own Scriptures that I have felt the inner compulsion to bear witness on behalf of what is true in Hinduism while writing this book.

There is a folk song of the Indian people, dearly loved by Mahatma Gandhi, which he has often wished to hear sung to him in the most sacred moments of his life. It is called the *Song of the True Vaishnava*. It gives, in a few words, the charac-

[1] See Chapter 6, p. 75.

ter which devout Vaishnava Hindus are taught from childhood to love and respect, and may be translated thus:—

> He is the true Vaishnava who knows and feels another's woes as his own.
> Ever ready to serve, he never boasts.
> He bows to every one and despises no one, keeping his thought, word, and deed pure.
> Blessed is the mother of such an one. He reverences every woman as his mother.
> He keeps an equal mind and does not stain his lips with falsehood; nor does he touch another's wealth.
> No bonds of attachment can hold him.
> Ever in tune with Ramanama, his body possesses in itself all places of pilgrimage.
> Free from greed and deceit, passion and anger, this is the true Vaishnava.

The remarkable thing is this: that there runs through it an inner resemblance to the special qualities which are given in St. Paul's Hymn of Charity, where Christian love is said to suffer long and to be kind, to have no envy and to be in no way puffed up. Therefore it has been painful to me to read some of the grossly ignorant statements which have appeared in Western literature, making out that Hinduism is nothing else than an obscene disease. A religion that can draw such a picture of goodness as the *Song of the True Vaishnava* and can produce living witnesses of its character like Mahatma Gandhi is worthy of all respect by any lover of the truth.

There is one further aspect of the Hindu religion

which is unfamiliar in the West, and also difficult to explain. Hinduism is a complete social system as well as a spiritual faith, and these two factors are so intimately combined that they can hardly be separated. Caste and along with it the whole social attitude towards marriage are intimately bound up together. They are *Dharma* (religious duty).

Perhaps on the question of marriage there is a common meeting-ground where the two religions stand together, and therefore it is easier for the West to visualize at that point what Hinduism always represents. For the Christian Church has brought marriage within the sphere of religion just as Hinduism has done. It is a sacrament in both cases. The religious sanction has been given to marriage as an indissoluble bond.

But what the Christian religion has made sacred in this one respect Hinduism has applied to every side of life, so that it is practically true that each act of the daily life to a strict Hindu must have the full sanction of religion. That this leads to constant abuses is evident. For human life is never static, and the changes made by time are often revolutionary. There is thus the terrible danger always present in outward observances of their becoming mistaken for the worship of the living God in spirit and in truth. Here the reformed Christian faith has surely much to offer of spiritual value to the East.

Yet behind all these outward observances Hinduism has sustained among countless men and women the thirst for the one God who is beyond all form. There has also been kept alive the noble conception that, as human life draws to its close, these outward forms may be laid aside, and men and women may retire from the activities of the world so that they may rely on God alone. This ideal of human existence is called the Four *Asrams*. After the period of the *Brahmachari*, which has to be kept in perfect continence, the stage of the *Grihastha*, or householder, is entered, during which the married life is lived in the midst of the social order. Still later there are two further stages to be passed through, called the *Vanaprastha* and *Sannyas*, wherein retirement from the world becomes more and more complete, until every tie that binds the soul to earth is broken as death approaches.

It is true that very few in these modern days keep these stages as they used to be kept of old, but the ideal of the four *asrams*, or stages of life, is deeply embedded in Hinduism and represents a very noble aspect of the Hindu religion.

It has only been possible in this brief chapter to deal for a moment with some points where the Western reader might be able to gain touch with Hinduism in a sympathetic manner. Other aspects of Hinduism have come up before us in other chapters. For in all this literature recently published, condemning Indian morals, the attack has really been directed, not so much against India, as against Hinduism as a religion; and those of us who have had intimate experience of the higher side of that religion, in such noble characters as Gandhi and Tagore, are in honour bound to defend it against such wholly one-sided imputations as these books represent.

Chapter 17

THE HINDU-MUSLIM QUESTION

THE contrasts on the surface between Hinduism and Islam are apparent. They form one of the chief difficulties now standing in the way of Indian national unity.

Hinduism accepts whole-heartedly the worship of the One Supreme—the "One without a second," the *Advaita*[1]—but at the same time allows the worshipper to employ pictures, symbols, images: Islam rejects idols altogether and will not allow pictures of any kind in any place of worship. Hinduism is in some ways like the Roman Catholicism of the south of Europe in its sacramental use of the material elements, reaching down from the beauty of flower offerings to much lower types: Islam is sternly "puritan," so that not even a flower must be seen within a mosque where prayer is offered and where the word of God is recited. Hinduism makes its appeal to the multitude of ordinary people by means of music, religious processions, festivals, and elaborate ritual: Islam is so austere that music is altogether prohibited at the time of prayer. Hinduism, once more, makes room for a Pantheon of deities in its conception of the Unseen and the Eternal: Islam, stark and bare from the Arabian desert, has avoided from the very first metaphysical

[1] i e. without duality.

subtleties and speculations about the divine nature, while it insists with tremendous emphasis on the pure, majestic unity of God, the All-merciful, the Compassionate, the Almighty.

Two dear old friends of mine in Delhi, long since dead, who could both of them remember the last of the Moghul Emperors and his court in Delhi, held contrary views concerning Islam in India in relation to Hinduism. The former, Maulvi Nazir Ahmad, the great Urdu novelist and theologian, would tell me, in his extreme old age when we talked together, that he saw absolutely no means of any final reconciliation between two religions so diverse as Hinduism and Islam. The second, Munshi Zaka Ullah, an Urdu prose writer and historian, who had spent a long lifetime of intellectual friendship both in Delhi and Allahabad with Hindu scholars and thinkers, held firmly the view, right up to the day of his death at the advanced age of eighty-seven, that harmony and reconciliation were always possible.

In much of the anti-Indian literature which has been published in the West a marked tendency has been noticeable to emphasize in an altogether one-sided manner the crudities of popular Hinduism, which are only too apparent on the surface, with a view to making good and sincere people believe that because these two religions are mutually antagonistic the presence of the third party, the British, is always necessary in India to prevent their adherents from cutting each other's throats.

The argument put forward has been usually of a

partisan character, with a preference for Islam and a scarcely veiled contempt for Hinduism. In India the phrase of Sir Bamfylde Fuller, that Islam was "the favourite wife," will not easily be forgotten. This partisanship was most marked in Miss Mayo's latest book, called *The Face of Mother India*, which was profusely illustrated with photographs reproduced in such a way as to show the baser aspects of Hinduism. The book, as I have stated, was proscribed; for it could only have stirred up the bitterest feelings and led to embittered controversy.

I have given elsewhere an account of the national volunteer work in North Bengal, where Hindu volunteers risked their lives to help the Muslim village people. This ought to prove to anyone who seeks to know the truth that beneath the surface there is a fund of deep common human sympathy where the two religions do really meet, even among the illiterate villagers, and that true brotherly feeling is there all the time. In a book recently published on the North-West Frontier I have written these words: "After thirty-three years' experience in every part of India, my own confirmed belief is that the rioting of recent years has been due to temporary excitement over political issues rather than to deep-seated and inveterate causes which can never be removed. I would, at the same time, fully recognize the fact that those religious differences always have existed and will continue. But they need not lead to bloodshed."[1]

[1] *The Challenge of the North-West Frontier*, published by Allen & Unwin Ltd., p. 139.

This direct personal experience, which I have tried to express in carefully measured terms, has been brought home to me in perspective through a study of Indian history, especially that of the Middle Ages in the East. Wherever there was a common meeting ground in mystical religious experience between Hinduism and Islam the result has been marvellously fruitful. The very contrasts between the two religions have had their notable values. For history plainly shows how the hard, aggressive, militant character of those who came from Central Asia and invaded India was softened by contact with Hinduism. On the other hand, Hindu civilization itself, in the long run, became benefited by its constant touch with Islam.

Let us work out together the historical process. The comparative purity of Hindu worship in the north is very noticeable, especially after anyone has visited the large temples of southern India, such as that at Madura. Again, we have seen already how the general treatment of the depressed classes in the north differs from that of the south. I shall not easily forget the shock I received in this direction when I first came down from the north and visited the Malabar coast. All this difference is not a little due to the presence of a faith, such as Islam, which swept aside much of the luxuriant ritual growth that had encumbered the worship of the one true God and insisted at the same time that, in the presence of the Lord of all creation, those who are created by Him of whatever race are equal.

But how much also does Islam owe in return! Let me tell one beautiful story that reveals Hinduism at its highest point, so far as I, an outsider, am able to judge it. Some time ago, at Santiniketan, I had been in the habit each morning of plucking a few white, scented blossoms and giving them to the poet, Rabindranath Tagore, for his writing-table before he began his day's work. But his daughter said to her father, "Why does he pluck the flowers when they are growing in the sunshine? Tell him not to do so. God gives us the blossoms when they fall. Let him gather *those* for his morning gift to you! They will provide you with the same beauty and perfume."

This deep sentiment, that does not wish anything, however humble, to be sacrificed to man's need, is one of the noblest things in Hinduism. It goes by the name of *Ahimsa*, which means "doing no harm." The contrast between this and the rough spirit of the militant invaders who entered India as conquerors from Central Asia runs through many pages of mediaeval Indian history. The weakness of Hinduism is on the surface, but it has deep down a moral strength which humanity could never afford to lose.

In the year 1936 I was privileged to spend many days at Mahatma Gandhi's village home in Central India, at a time when Khan Abdul Gaffar Khan was staying with him. He is one of the noblest Muslims I have ever met, as tender as a child and as brave as a lion. There I saw a picture of Hindu-Muslim unity which I shall always remember. Each was learning from the other about things human and divine, and I was learning precious lessons also. From the Khan Sahib himself I learnt especially concerning the higher bravery of suffering as an essential feature of Islam, because the Prophet in the days of his rejection and persecution had placed his faith in God and God alone. All the saints and prophets, he said to me, had been persecuted. It was the way in which God purified them in the fire of suffering until the dross was burnt away and they came out at last pure gold. "Look at your Prophet," he said to me, "how He was persecuted to the very end."

In the Middle Ages the great saints of Hinduism, as far away from one another as Bengal in the east is distant from Sind in the west, made the most earnest effort to appreciate Islam. They interpreted the Unity of God in terms of the Upanishads. Caste and idolatry meant very little to such men of religion. They treated all those around them, of whatever creed, as brothers and sisters, and sought to break down the barrier of untouchability altogether. They paid such reverence to the saints of Islam that the Sufi devotees, who were mystics, welcomed in turn the Hindu philosophy presented to them by the Hindu saints and appropriated some of their ideas. So closely did they draw near to one another that the songs of these men of God on either side are still sung by Hindus and Muslims alike in the villages of northern India.

Thus while brutal fighting was going on between kings and princes the village folk were finding a harmony which would bring them near to God. But the harsh orthodoxies on either side have again and again thrown things back into riot and confusion. Wild passions have been excited which have swept like a fire across the country. When these have burnt themselves out, they have left a track of shame behind them. It needs to be remembered that the number of those in the villages who have had any education at all is very small. Thus rumour gets a hold upon ignorant minds and inflames passionate emotions.

I have tried, with all sincerity, to describe this vast religious background of village life in northern India, where the numbers of the adherents of Hinduism and Islam are far more evenly balanced than in the south. How these strong discrepancies will end, no one can possibly foretell. But just as in Europe the cruel wars of religion between Protestant and Catholic of three centuries ago burnt themselves out, so it may happen in India. Indeed, among the greater part of those who are nationally minded a common meeting place has already been found.

One anxiety that I have already mentioned has been much in my mind of late. It is whether a subtle secularism may not supersede the deep religious spirit which is still strong in modern India; whether there may not be a depreciation of the true spirit of religion itself; whether, in despising the dead superstitions of the past, the very soul of religion may be lost sight of. Such a loss would be a supreme disaster, because this true spirit of religion is the highest that man can aspire to, even though he may never be able to attain. Recently, the external and the material have so occupied men's minds that the inward and spiritual have fallen into sad neglect. The age of politics almost inevitably tends towards a secular view of human life.

Young India, copying Soviet Russia far too closely, and leaving on one side the fountain-head of truth in the immortal sayings of its own past, has been ready to throw over religion altogether and turn the whole main purpose of life into the economic struggle. But those of us who have known and revered those great souls, few in number, whose lives were devoted entirely to God's service, can never disown the faith and goodness which we saw proceeding from them; for its spiritual beauty was transparent.

Chapter 18

INDIAN CHARACTER

YOUNG INDIA would be the first to blame me if I gave merely what might be called an apologetic or laudatory account of Indian moral character without speaking the truth about the very serious evils which have sapped in the past the national life and still do serious mischief. These evils are often very different from those which hostile critics have placarded in the West. Let us face them together, as far as I have been able to see them, with a critical but kindly eye.

One of the greatest faults, which has become ingrained owing to centuries of subjection, and is still there beneath the surface, is the habit of submissiveness and apathy in face of wrong, instead of its fearless, active condemnation. That is why untouchability and a thousand other evils have not been brought to an end long ago. That is why men of kindly nature, who have had the power in their own hands, have allowed women terribly to suffer. That is why gross superstition, leading to all manner of cruel fears, has been permitted to go on without any persistent effort on the part of men of high intelligence to remove it. That is why, in a land where love of animals is present in a marked degree, the most horrible tortures have been allowed to continue without the enlightened Indian public rising up in wrath against them. A social conscience is beginning to be formed at last, but why has it been so feeble during all these centuries? I know well from my own experience that the enervating heat of India has much to answer for, and the after-effects of malaria are terribly weakening. But it is altogether wrong to make such things as these a plausible excuse for doing nothing at all. The religious life of India seems for some reason to have lacked driving power; otherwise that noble reverence for the animal creation which Hinduism professes could never have gone on so long side by side with unspeakably cruel practices (such as *phooka*) in the midst of the wealthy and enlightened Hindu community of Calcutta and Bombay, and even at Benares itself. It is my own conviction, based on many years of experience in India, that centuries of subjection have done more in their harmfulness than either the lassitude due to climate or any other external cause.

This passive submission, when evil is being perpetrated, has gone deep beneath the surface. It seems to run through every section of the community, and to account also for the prolonged acquiescence in foreign rule and the willingness to leave all responsibility in foreign hands. While the contact between East and West, which came about through the British occupation, brought undoubted advantages, yet it served only to increase this submissive spirit and this lack of initiative. For this reason much of the good was neutralized as the years passed. On the one side there was the fault of the British rulers, who took upon themselves control of everything, and thus deprived highly capable Indians of the power and opportunity of serving their country in the most responsible positions. On the other side the blame rested upon Indians themselves for passively accepting such a humiliating situation, which led to their own increasing weakness. At one time it would even appear that they gloried in their shame and flattered their rulers to their hearts' content. Only very slowly indeed did a salutary change come about and a spirit of independence arise.

It is a matter of intense thankfulness to me to note, during the present year, 1938, how on the British side as well as the Indian this fundamental fault is being recognized at last and steps are being taken to overcome it. For in the provincial councils the British rulers are rapidly withdrawing from responsibility in a way they have never done before, and the Indian leaders are accepting it and making good. While these words are being written the new situation thus created appears to be full of hope in spite of occasional friction.

Robert Bridges, in his greatest poem, called *The Testament of Beauty*, has written some searching lines about the evil result of lack of self-assertion in a noble cause. These verses demand attention on the part of those who hold to the principle of non-violence, but have not realized at the same time the paramount need of steadfast moral resistance. He brings forward the Spartan general, Brasidas, who was amused at a tiny mouse when it ran out of a basket of figs and he tried to catch it. The mouse turned round suddenly and bit his hand, and the great general laughed at the pluck of the little creature. He laughed instead of getting angry with it. The poet writes:—

> I had disliked Brasidas, if he had killed that mouse.

Then he gives his own judgment in the following words, which will repay careful study:—

> For Brasidas held that courage ennobleth man,
> and from unworth redeemeth; and that folk who shrink
> from venture of battle in self-defence are thereby doomed
> to slavery and extinction; and so this mouse, albeit
> its little teeth had done him a petty hurt, deserved
> liberty for its courage, and found grace in man.

If we are permitted to take, as Robert Bridges would certainly allow us, the words "venture of battle" in a moral rather than a physical sense when speaking of civilized mankind, these words appear to me with aptness to apply to India herself at the present time. The leaders of Indian opinion, under the guidance of Mahatma Gandhi, have been discovering how exactly true they are. This has made the old mendicant policy of mere petitioning more and more intolerable to them. For, as Seeley the historian has put it, they have felt it "shameful to assist the foreigner in maintaining his dominion." This new national sentiment, thus realized on a large scale, has been the motive force in the whole non-co-operation movement. It is there still, ready to be called forth at any moment whenever needed.

There is, of course, all the difference in the world between apathetic submissiveness and the active soul-force of the true Satyagrahi (civil resister). The latter is fighting for freedom all the while, but he is using only moral weapons. He does not "shrink from the venture of battle in self-defence," as Robert Bridges puts it. He is really the bravest man alive—much braver than the savage fighter, who fights while his blood is hot with excitement, and often needs a stimulant to keep up his courage.

"The one who submits," says Mahatma Gandhi, "merely to save his own skin is a shirker and a coward." There is such a thing as soul-cowardice. Therefore Gandhi himself has always stigmatized this weakness as "slave mentality," and has declared that it strikes at the root of all high moral character. No one in India has done more than he has done, both by example and precept, to drive this evil out of the Indian mind for ever.

Here the recent political resisters, starting from a non-violent basis, have already won amazing victories. For it requires a brave man and a brave woman to face the ordeal of going to prison joyfully. Where, as in the last struggle, those who offered themselves thus unresistingly numbered more than a hundred thousand, including a large proportion of women, it may truly be said that the back of "slave mentality" was broken.

Not that, for many generations, the deepest roots

of this old inherited weakness and vice will be cut away; for they have spread too far underground and are likely to reappear. But those men and women who have been through the very severe ordeal of the late political struggle, under Mahatma Gandhi's leadership, will now stand out for what is right, both in municipal and provincial affairs, as soon as ever they assume responsibility. They are also likely to make steadfast national leaders.

There is another weakness, which has grown up during the centuries and has spread like a weed, side by side with the evil growth that I have already mentioned. If I write severely about this, I must be pardoned: for I have seen during many years the harm that it has constantly done, and I cannot write otherwise.

In India the family system, with its very intricate relationships, has been made the one end in life to work for, rather than public service. Alas! the evils which are bound up with subjection, over long centuries, have taken no heavier toll than this: that they have driven the most unselfish virtues downward into this inner circle of the family and have left the national life to look after itself and its functions to be performed by others. The same thing had happened also in China under the foreign Manchu dynasty, and it is still one of the greatest curses there to-day, leading to the constant taking of bribes for family aggrandisement even in face of public disaster. Only the tremendous danger from Japan has been able to loosen its hold.

Those who have left, for a century or more, the concerns of their own nation in the hands of others become almost inevitably introverted. When this happens, the concentration upon family interests leaves weaknesses behind of a very serious nature. Public interests suffer.

I do not wish for a moment to deny that there are qualities connected with this strong family interest which are noble and good. I have often been deeply moved to see the almost intolerable load of responsibility which members of the family will bear for one another. But when it *ends* there, and the wider interests become sacrificed for it, then surely it lacks that "magnanimity" which the Greeks and Romans so rightly admired.

This greatness of soul is seen expressed, in a tragic form, in the noble picture drawn of Arjuna in the Gita, where he is called upon to join battle *even against his own kith and kin* at the summons of a higher call. Christ taught this terribly severe lesson when He commanded His disciples that even father and mother and wife and child must be given up for the sake of the highest cause of all, which He named the Kingdom of God.

No doubt this is a hard saying; and gentle, loving men and women find it just as hard to-day as it was when it was first uttered. Yet it forms the refined material out of which saints and heroes are made, and human society will fall back into a mere animal existence if there are not those in each generation who are ready to carry out this supreme sacrifice for others. Fortunately, in India the religious appeal has hitherto had power in it to call men and women out from the narrow confinement of the home. Some of those who have obeyed the call have been the salt of the earth, without which human life would have lost its savour. Now the national appeal has come to reinforce the appeal which religion had made in the past. There will be political ascetics to-day as there were religious ascetics of old.

One serious consequence of the confined atmosphere, where the family rather than the nation is the final unit, has been the lack of cohesion and unity in any great public cause. Not only do the ties of the family prove too strong, but the public cause itself is left in abeyance for personal and family reasons. There enters in a lack of that discipline which every great cause supremely needs.

The way out of this vicious circle, whether in India or China, is for the whole family, wherever possible, to become imbued with the new spirit of national service so that each member is ready to make sacrifices.[1] Where this has not yet been found possible, the burden will fall most heavily on the younger generation; for there is an idealism in youth which tends to diminish with age.

This breaking loose from the rigid family bonds has already been splendidly demonstrated in India by the active service of the national volunteers. The different instances which I have given in an earlier chapter will prove how the mind of youth at the

[1] See Chapter 3, p. 51, for a signal example of this.

present juncture truly responds to this higher call of service.

Yet here again it may take many generations before the new spirit finds a wholly congenial soil in India itself wherein it may flourish. For after years of neglect it is a plant of slow growth unless the ground is carefully prepared.

A third obstacle, about which I have already written a great deal, is Caste. Let me say here very briefly that it has become clear to me, after a sympathetic study over a large number of years, that caste in modern India has lost its ancient values. In its present form, caste is doing harm to the life of the nation by dividing and separating man from man and family from family. No man can serve two masters. The ends that "Caste" and "Nation" serve are different. Since the subject is difficult for the West to grasp, I must be allowed here a little repetition.

No impartial historian would doubt that in the distant past caste possessed functions which were useful for the whole community and produced a congenial and equable social well-being. But when a rigid and inflexible religious taboo on freedom of marriage became bound up with caste itself as one of its main bulwarks, so that intermarriage led to cruel excommunication, then a form of segregation began which has made a cohesive national life well-nigh impossible. This process became more and more injurious as the number of sub-castes increased. It has now reached a point where it is the most serious danger to the community, as may be seen in the case of the excluded or scheduled castes. If these number in all one-seventh to one-sixth of the whole Indian population, as the last census appears to show, it may easily be seen what a serious wound has been dealt to the body politic.

Certainly an impartial historian, who would commend caste in its earlier form, would condemn it as it has now shown its evil features. For along with the misery of untouchability, the strict and rigid ban on intermarriage, even among the sub-castes, has increased the twin evils of child brides and child widows.

The Indian newspapers recently contained a paragraph, printed in bold type as important news, informing the public that in south India certain persons had been excommunicated and outcasted because they had taken part in what was called a "cosmopolitan tea party." This meant that because they had sought to maintain friendly relations of a hospitable character with their own fellow countrymen, who were not high-caste Hindus, they were to be turned out of Hindu society altogether. The insult was made worse by the declaration that if they did a humiliating penance for the offence they would be received back again!

No nation can ever be built up on those lines! Hindu-Muslim unity becomes impossible. The Muslim, Christian, and Hindu can never really work together where such distinctions are kept. The hateful cry at the railway stations, "*Hindu Pani*,"

"*Musalman Pani*" ("Hindu water," "Musalman water") is surely one that must bring a deep sense of shame to every true lover of his country. God gives us water to drink and air to breathe, and we are insulting Him when we claim exclusive rights. All this segregation and aloofness ought to have been done away with long ago. It is stupid and foolish, as well as palpably inhuman. Moreover, it is utterly illogical to object to segregation in South Africa while keeping up this inner segregation in India itself.

How was it ever possible (this question has to be faced) for Hinduism to present a united front before the invader, who came into India from Central Asia with a small but compact body of men united by a common bond, when segregation had already been sanctioned in the name of religion and any revolt from such a bondage was regarded as a deadly sin? Under modern conditions such regulations are unthinkable! They have no moral meaning. They could never stand the strain of war. At any crisis they either break down, or else lead on to humiliating defeat.

I have just been reading through the account of the destruction of Jerusalem which is told at length by the Jewish writer Josephus. The one thing that helped the Roman legions most of all to conquer the holy city was the utter disunion within the walls. For the Jews themselves had long been divided into different religious factions. The analogy is far from exact; but it will serve its purpose to show what must happen when religion divides man from his fellow man instead of binding men together. If India is ever to be a united nation, very drastic changes in the whole caste system will have to be made, and there must be no trifling with the evil.

Here the right direction has been shown by Mahatma Gandhi. With true courage and humanity, he has first of all adopted an "untouchable" child as his own daughter. Thus he has broken down for ever the greatest of all caste barriers. Furthermore, he has welcomed with joy and thankfulness the intercaste marriage of his son with the daughter of C. Rajagopalachariar, a Brahmin, who belongs to a caste entirely different from that of Gandhi himself. By this happy event two families which had taken the lead in the national cause were united by marriage, and all India rejoiced over it. Such a drastic action has shown how ready for reform the public mind is, if only a right lead is given to it. The old functional ideal of caste may still be preserved in many ways, but the restrictions on intercaste marriage must be removed. Only thus can true national unity be attained.

With regard to Islam in India, there is not the same need to write at length as I have done about Hinduism. For it is a well-proved historical fact that by far the larger proportion of Muslims in India are of Hindu extraction. In their village life they still retain many of the old weaknesses from which Hindus suffer, especially in East Bengal. At the same time, Islam itself as a religion has essentially a democratic outlook, because all men are equal beneath the sovereign power of God. This dignity of outlook and equality of bearing will probably make it less difficult in the long run for the Muslims to advance with the times and throw aside outworn customs. There is a pathway always open for advance, if only religious intolerance can be overcome.

But at present a deplorable lack of education stands right in the way of immediate progress. This, more than anything else, has kept back the Muslim community as a body—numbering nearly one-fourth of the population—from fulfilling its proper functions and taking its rightful and proper place in the life of the nation. As this educational backwardness passes away and the younger generation comes to the front, there is every hope that Hindu-Muslim co-operation will come nearer to fulfilment. Those tendencies to hold aloof, which have so painfully revealed themselves in the past, will die a natural death.

There is one aspect of modern life in India that has troubled me, not only among Muslims, but also among Hindus, and I would venture to emphasise it still further. The sense of dependence upon God, which was the strength of the older generation in both religions, appears somehow to have lost its power. The moral sanctions of a good life are likely to be weakened if this tendency becomes more pronounced; for man cannot live by bread alone; and economics apart from religion make slender fare for the spirit of man to feed on, however important the economic solution of India's ills may be.

Among Indian Christians, who have hitherto in the past been taken freely into Government service, a parting of the ways has come. Great decisions will have to be made about the future. Instead of the comparative ease in gaining employment which availed them in the past, a much harder life will now lie in front of them. They will often have to struggle with hard poverty and surrender a privileged position. But this, in the long run, is likely to strengthen their inner character just in the very place where before it was weak. For only as the Indian Christian Church accepts the full responsibility of its own self-government and learns there the democratic spirit will it be able on the one hand to take its full part in the life of the nation, and at the same time to show with equal clearness the practice of the fundamental precepts of the Sermon on the Mount.

The Anglo-Indians, who are of mixed descent and have English blood in their veins, are in the most difficult position of all. They are being drawn both ways at once. The tendency to cling to the British side is naturally very strong indeed. Their own leading men, however, are fully aware of the vast changes which are being made before their eyes, and they can understand the urgent need to offer freely and whole-heartedly full allegiance to the country in which they were born. Those Indian leaders who are now responsible Ministers in the provinces are anxious to win their support. Therefore the future is hopeful, if only they are ready to accept the clear verdict of facts and come into the full tide of Indian national life.

The Parsees are a small community chiefly centred in Bombay. They have remarkably kept their own character and independence, and have also given men of sterling worth, like Dadabhai Naoroji and Sir Pherozeshah Mehta, to the national cause. They alone have never asked for any special consideration at the Round Table Conferences. Indeed, it would be readily conceded that they have won their present position by their generous public service.

In this very brief sketch I have not mentioned separately the religious reforming bodies, such as the Sikh community, the Brahmo Samaj, the Arya Samaj, and the Ramakrishna Mission, because they have themselves already initiated important moral reforms and their support may be counted on in favour of all that makes for social progress.

In concluding this chapter, I would refer in as few words as possible to a personal experience which has made India doubly dear to me. The affection which has been given to me by the people in the villages has touched me more than I can possibly describe. No more gentle, peace-loving, and tender-hearted people exist on this earth than these Indian villagers. Nowhere else in the world could I have found such deep personal love and have been enabled to return it. It has also been my singular good fortune to make lifelong friendships with Muslims and Hindus alike, as well as within the Christian community to which I belong. If I had my life to live over again, I would wish to spend it once more in India.

Chapter 19

THE UNITY OF INDIA

It has almost become an axiom with a certain class of statesmen in the West that India has no cohesion of its own, and that only the might of the British arm prevents an immediate disruption from taking place. India, they tell us, is a sub-continent rather than an organized nation. It is, they say, merely made up of a conglomeration of races and tribes and peoples, which have never been welded together into a single whole. It has, they often repeat, more than one hundred and forty different languages, and its religions are so diverse and contradictory that the people would literally tear one another to pieces if once the strong arm of British rule were withdrawn.

Mr. Lloyd George used this plausible but erroneous theory when he made his famous speech comparing the Indian Civil Service to a steel frame that could never be removed. The whole structure, he asserted, which had been so laboriously welded together by the British rulers, would immediately collapse if that steel frame were ever withdrawn.

Others have used the same argument, and it lies at the back of much that has been written by authors whose subconscious desire is to retain at all costs the people of India within the framework of British rule. They dwell specially on the law and order maintained by the British Raj and cemented by the English language which is the *lingua franca* spoken to-day throughout the country. The tiny body of English-speaking civilians, with the British Army behind them, are, according to this school, the only unifiers of the country.

With regard to the past century, it would be freely admitted that the common law and administration did much to create the beginnings of a nation-wide movement, but all historians of eminence agree on one point that a spiritual unity had already given a background to the whole structure.

The language difficulty is by no means as insoluble as people have been led to imagine. In spite of the fact that India is a continent as big and as populous as the whole of Western Europe, it is singularly fortunate in the simplicity of its language question. For it is quite easy to find out, as I have done by actual experience, how very seldom human intercourse is blocked by any obstacle of language difference. Instead of the "hundred and forty odd languages," which are often spoken of by controversialists, the main vehicles of speech in India are remarkably few. The only sharp division is between the northern and the southern groups. For the northern languages are mainly Sanskritic, and the southern are mainly Dravidian. But even here the Sanskrit element in the southern group is important and an Indian *lingua franca* should not be difficult of attainment.

There is one further problem of language which

is acute in the north at the present time. For there the two different religious cultures of Hinduism and Islam have to be carefully considered, as they carry with them certain language differences. The Muslim naturally looks back to the familiar Persian words, which were common speech under the Moghul Emperors and were successfully blended with Hindi, forming the mixed language called Urdu. Hindi and Urdu have now both found their own natural areas in the north of India. The only question that remains is how they may be enabled to intermingle in common, everyday conversation and spread also to the south. For this purpose, what is now called "Hindustani" is likely to become the most popular medium for daily intercourse and to extend its use all over India among merchants, travellers, and pilgrims.

I have very little doubt that such a genuine working language, with a number of very common basic words and a minimum of grammar, will soon take the place of English in ordinary conversation and in the end become the common speech of India. It need not produce a literature, but it may one day be sufficiently widespread to serve the purpose of the wayfarers through the villages of India, where English is entirely unknown. If such a prediction comes true, this common speech will take shape naturally, and not by learned discussions about it. The Hindi pedant, with his long string of Sanskrit words, and the learned Maulvi, with his equally abstruse Arabic, can never artificially compose a language for daily employment in the market-place. For such a speech is like the small coin in common use, well rubbed and worn, the medium of ordinary conversation, rather than a high literary language to be read only in books.

Also to-day we have to think of the new prospects of unification which the inventions of modern science, such as the wireless, bring nearer to our doors. While the English language is still only understood by a small number of intellectuals, this growing common language, called "Hindustani," is already becoming easily followed by two hundred and fifty million people in the north and centre. Even in the south, where the Dravidian languages are spoken, a smattering of this northern speech has already become familiar. Here at Tirupattur Asram, in the Madras Presidency, I can already distinguish as I hear them the northern Sanskrit words, which have become intermingled with the Tamil. Yesterday, when I tried to speak in English to one who had called in to see me, he said to me, "Please speak in Hindustani," and when I spoke in that language he easily followed what I had to say.

Broadcasting, the talkies, the rapidly growing newspaper press, compulsory primary education of boys and girls which may soon be established, huge inter-provincial conferences furnished with loud-speakers—all these modern contrivances are levelling large areas of human intercourse till a much wider audience is being obtained. Very soon mere dialects will survive only as curiosities. None but the larger languages will remain; and along with them a *lingua franca* will become a necessity.

So fully is this modern utilitarian idea of language becoming grasped by those in popular authority that the President of the All-India National Congress has frankly advised that the example of modern Turkey should be followed and the Roman script be universally employed, in order to unify the country still further and to make primary education easier for the young children. Such a proposal made in a Presidential Congress speech, even a year ago, would probably have raised a sharp and bitter controversy. But to-day it has met with little opposition. The tide is running very fast and great things are happening.

But far beyond this new unification, which is likely more and more to be brought about by language, there is, as I have related, a deeper unity which has always been present in India and has been recognized by such conservative historians as Dr. Vincent Smith and others. It goes back for thousands of years and owes its origin in history to the remarkable cultural process which took place in Vedic times embodying pre-Vedic ideas. The spiritual atmosphere that was then created—first of all in the Punjab, and afterwards in the Ganges Valley—spread by degrees towards the south.

The Buddhist and Jain movements, which at one time covered the whole of India, gave to this spiritual atmosphere the commanding religious conception of *Ahimsa*, or non-violence. Climate and the human mind conspired together to produce a peaceful spirit which has been rarely found to the same extent in any other region of the world. China received it from India through Mahayana Buddhism and found it equally congenial to her own civilization. Thus one vast area, more populous than any other part of the globe, became "civilized" in the best sense of the word.

Not merely did this atmosphere of *Ahimsa* spread a humane ideal wherever it went; it also made India one people. So strong has been its influence that Islam, which came to India later from Central Asia, tended to lose by slow degrees some of its earlier belligerent aspects. It felt that peace within which the name "Islam" implies.[1]

Thus every nomad tribe or conquering race that entered India received something of the spirit of the country, the *genius loci*, which every thoughtful person who lives in India for any length of time recognizes and understands.

To sum up the facts which this chapter has outlined in brief, neither by differences of language nor race nor religion has there been as yet such a pronounced cleavage in India as to imply that the presence of a third party, such as the British, is perpetually needed in order to keep the peace. Whatever differences there are have been steadily overcome; and the century of outward peace under the British occupation has helped to bring together and make familiar with one another the diverse

[1] The root meaning of Islam is "peace."

provinces. A unity has now been inaugurated which is likely to grow stronger and will not need continual propping up from the outside. Those who witnessed the vast Congress gathering at Haripura, where friction was reduced to a minimum and a spirit of unity prevailed throughout, can have little doubt that Indians from all the provinces are learning that discipline from within which is essential for all true national life.

If the Indian States, with their personal and autocratic rule, be pointed to as a perpetual dividing line across the map of India, the answer may be given that this division of India has been kept intact hitherto by the British power alone. The withdrawal of that power is therefore not likely to increase any division on the map which already exists. Indeed, a change of government may help to remove the anomaly of as many as six hundred states maintained apart from the provinces by an alien power.

While there are large numbers in the West who desire intensely that India should be free and independent, there are some among them who have hitherto quite honestly been forced by what they have read to believe that such a goal is very far distant. They do not accept in this case the truth of the proverb *solvitur ambulando*, which might be paraphrased as implying that the exercise of freedom begets freedom, and the use of self-government promotes the sense of responsibility. No one contemplates a hurried or immediate withdrawal at a moment's notice, but on the other hand no Indian can contemplate with equanimity the entrenchment of British rule at the centre as if it were destined to last for ever. The real danger has been that responsibility has hitherto been given too late instead of too soon. But the remedy for this is surely not to insist on its being held back still longer. It rather points to the handing over of responsibility wherever and whenever this can be done. Along that adventurous path the future of India lies.

Chapter 20

THE TWO CIVILIZATIONS

THOSE who come out to the East from Europe and America have often great difficulty in understanding at first what heavy encumbrances an ancient civilization is obliged to carry with it owing to the accumulations of the past which cannot be thrown off quickly without losing precious treasure in the process.

Northern Europe and America are both comparatively modern. They represent a New World, which, in mechanical contrivance and scientific invention, has gone far beyond the ancient civilizations of the East. One of the most pressing dangers, at the present time, lies in the fact that material power is rapidly passing out of the hands of these older civilizations before the New World has attained that riper wisdom which would enable it to appreciate the gathered heritage of the past. The vandalism within England itself, whereby beautiful old villages are being destroyed, is an example on a minute scale of what is happening all over the earth to-day.

Europe and America have yet to learn reverence in their treatment of other races. They may have cleared away some of the surface evils, but they have not yet learnt to control those unruly passions of violence within which lead on to the plunder of other people. They have heaped up riches and stored them, saying, "Soul, take thine ease," but they have not had time to listen to the voice of God, saying, "Thou fool! This night shall thy soul be required of thee." There has not yet come to the West the supreme courage of a great renunciation in answer to the haunting question which Christ Himself has set before us: "What shall it profit a man, if he gain the whole world and lose his own soul, or what shall a man give in exchange for his soul?"

The habitable earth on which we live is growing smaller every day. The civilizations—old and young—are clashing at every point. There ought to be mutual accommodation and a recognition of each other's contribution to the good of the whole. But for the West, in its arrogance, to "bestride the world like a Colossus," solely because of its material power, would mean a betrayal of what is highest and best in human affairs. It would also mean a rejection of the true wealth which the East still preserves for the future benefit of mankind.

In many respects the Western people—especially in the colder north—had the good fortune to start within a new geographical area, untrammelled by the impediments of the past. They began, as it were, with a clean slate. Very little had to be rubbed off in order to make room for the new. But the ancient East, where long ages of civilization had already gone by, had sent its own roots of culture deep down into the soil; and while there were weeds which had to be cleared away, there was also a priceless growth. This culture of the East represented the mature wisdom of quiet leisure and retirement—the fruit of slow and measured thought. The West, with its impetuous haste, has hitherto done very little either to respect or value this treasure which the East has still in store. There has been, quite lately, placarded instead before the eyes of men a shallow and contemptuous picture of Indian morals, whose untruth I have tried to expose in this book. Such a view of India is far too self-righteous, either to sympathize or to understand: it is also bound up with a fierce and unreasoning racial pride which carries with it all the haughtiness of the conqueror towards the conquered.

India had been unable in the past to resist the invasions of foreigners who came from the outside to rule over her. But even in her darkest hour, she had sought by her own innate genius to rise above this outward defeat and live in the realm of the spirit. Subdued on the worldly plane, she had still retained her own idealism intact. Yet, just when she felt the new urge of spiritual life coursing through her veins, an attack has been levelled against her by those writers who have never known the secret of her greatness. By gross exaggeration of her weaknesses, which are on the surface, she has been made out to be a "pariah" among the nations, whose very touch is contaminating on account of filthy habits and sexual perversions. No more cruel attack than this could have been made at such a time. It has created an entire misunderstanding in the West of the one country which, at the present crisis, has a peculiar heritage of truth to give to mankind. It has prevented India's contribution to world peace from receiving the favourable hearing it deserved.

The assumption by the West of racial superiority, lying behind this cruel attack, is a double-edged weapon which turns back like a knife on the hand that uses it. India has felt this wound in a way that no insult has ever hurt her sensitive spirit before. She has made her appeal to a higher power than that of man, and it will not be made in vain.

The words of Christ, in the Sermon on the Mount, need to be carefully remembered by the West to-day:—

> Judge not, that ye be not judged.
> For with what judgment ye judge, ye shall be judged:
> And with what measure ye meet
> It shall be measured to you again.
> And why beholdest thou the mote that is in thy brother's eye,
> And considerest not the beam which is in thine own eye?
> Thou hypocrite!
> First cast out the beam out of thine own eye:
> And then thou shalt see clearly
> To cast out the mote which is in thy brother's eye.

Step by step, with incredibly humiliating defeat, Europe has been forced to re-examine her own presumptuous claims to superior wisdom. As the years have gone by, since the Great War, she has found the moral foundations giving way beneath her. For she has become entangled in a net of ever-increasing violence from which she has vainly tried to extricate herself. The sins of past generations, whereby she exploited the rest of the earth for her own gain, have now been brought home to her by the hopeless waste of armaments piled on armaments, until another world conflict seems hardly to be avoided. Every frantic attempt to escape from this vicious circle has hitherto only driven her farther forward along the road to ruin.

Meanwhile in the face of ever-impending disaster a way of life, singularly "Christian" in its conception, is being set forward by Mahatma Gandhi, who is himself not a Christian but a Hindu. It is acted out by many thousands of his followers, who have been ready along with him to suffer imprisonment and face death itself rather than surrender their faith. His aim has been to establish in the hearts of men non-violence and truth, fearlessly practised, as the simple, necessary means of overcoming violence and untruth. How far he will succeed history alone can show: but nowhere in the world is there any prospect for the future which has such a gleam of hope as this.

For in India the ground has already been prepared. From the time of the Buddha onward the taking of life has been held to be instinctively abhorrent over large areas of the country. The climate itself, with its spaces of quiet, has encouraged a peaceful view of human existence. This geographical factor has to be taken into account, as well as the dynamic personalities of such men as Gandhi and Tagore. The peace-lover in India, who is ready to die for the cause rather than commit violence, has surely a vitally true message for the tempestuous north, where even to live at all means conflict. Whatever the ultimate cause may be, it should be counted for righteousness that in this central position in Asia one-fifth of the human race has already stood out for peace, and still stands out for it under Mahatma Gandhi's leadership to-day. Cannot the West make use of this treasure that is thus being put into her own hands?

My point is made, if I am able to win from my own countrymen and those in America, to whom this book is mainly addressed, a deep reverence for Indian civilization as a whole. It may be that for many years to come there will continue to be wide differences between us, but that is no reason why there should not be also a growing sympathy and understanding; for true and lasting friendship depends more than anything else on mutual good-will. The world stands sorely in need of friendship, and a continued effort must be made from both sides to attain it, while all around us the passions which make for war are being exploited by every devilish ingenuity that science has been able to devise.

Many civilizations have perished; yet India and China remain. They are old, and yet they have been able to renew their youth. They are changing before our eyes, but their pace is different from that of the West; and to force the pace will do more harm than good. For whatever change is permanent must come from within. There is a patience in India and China that often puts us younger people of the West to shame. They take the longer view; and in consequence, when rapid changes are being made, they survive.

This slow process of the East often troubles us beyond words. Whenever our impatience is generous and sincere, it may do good rather than harm, and encourage the much-needed reform. But if we would be truly helpful, we must first judge ourselves. We must not condemn "untouchability" in India, and leave on one side the negro problem within our own borders. We must not pass a judgment on Kalighat, and leave unnoticed the inhumanities of our own butchers' shambles. We must not pour scorn on the East for cruelties towards animals, and look on with unconcern while animals are being trapped by hateful devices in the West. Again and again we come back to Christ's words: "Judge not, that ye be not judged."

There is often a pathetic look of old age and ancient wisdom in the faces of tiny children in India. I have seen it in China also. Compared with the chubby babies in the new civilizations of the cold north that look so physically content, these Indian children are marvellously winsome and attractive; yet there is something that often "lies too deep for tears" in the vast antiquity that seems to lie behind them.

Ill-health may partly account for this appearance of old age both in mother and child: for one must never forget the cruel effects of malaria and other tropical diseases, which are in the bloodstream. Yet with all her handicaps of climate and disease, India has marvellously revived. The deep roots of her culture have remained secure in the soil and have thrown up vigorous shoots above the ground. These have borne fresh leaves and flowers and fruit even in our own day. This should surely win the respect and even the reverence of the West, just as a mother is revered by her younger children.

The antiquity of India, which I have stressed, as contrasted with the youth of Europe is not a mere metaphor. It is one of the most significant facts of human history, and it reaches down into that realm of the Unconscious wherefrom the stuff of Thought is drawn. It marks a difference which is always there; and it should surely prevent any hasty judgment being formed from the side of the West. The grace of humility in this regard has been badly needed in the past; and at least in the present crisis of Europe, when the very foundations appear to be giving way, the presumptuous claim of the West to pre-eminence should be abated.

If what I have here stated is carefully borne in mind, then the corollary follows that a country like India, which, in spite of all these difficulties, has continued to produce age after age its own art, music, and literature, together with flashes of religious insight, cannot possibly be rotten at the core. Only an evil tree brings forth evil fruit: a good tree brings forth good fruit. The world verdict here is quite unchallengeable: and India has already received such a world verdict in her own favour. For it has been very widely acknowledged in the West that two at least of the greatest moral pioneers in the world to-day are Gandhi and Tagore. Surely a country with such a progeny cannot be called morally bankrupt!

Babylon, Nineveh, Tyre—what are they to-day as compared with India and her immortal youth, which blossoms even in old age?

When historical considerations such as these are brought to notice, they make any taunts from the West concerning India's decadence appear vulgar and cheap. Her long annals are recorded, not merely in decades, but in centuries.

Constant thoughts upon this age-long problem of East and West have been at the back of my own mind while I have been writing this book; and I have been testing them out one by one. It has been good to go over the ground again in order to see where the weakness both of Eastern and Western civilizations lies, as well as to review their strength. For the cheering thing to-day is this: that India has faced resolutely the worst of her internal evils. She has taken up the task of her own renewal, and will not lay it down.

Appendix I

TAGORE'S LETTER

THE poet Rabindranath Tagore wrote to *The Nation*, London, as follows:—

SIR,—I came to know from the advertising columns of your paper that Miss Katherine Mayo's *Mother India* has been lauded by Arnold Bennett as a "shocking book, in the honourable sense." Unfortunately, for obvious reasons, there is a widely prevalent wish among the race that rules India to believe any detraction that may bring discredit upon India, and consequently the kind of shocks that Miss Mayo has manufactured offers them a delicious luxury of indignation. The numerous lies mixed with facts that have been dexterously manipulated by her for the production of these shocks are daily being exposed in our journals; but these will never reach the circle of readers which it is easy for Miss Mayo to delude. Along with other Eastern victims of lying propaganda we in India also must defencelessly suffer mud-smearing from unscrupulous literature; for your writers have their machinery of publicity which is cruelly efficient for raining slanders from a region usually unapproachable by us, shattering our fair name in an appealingly wholesale manner.

I happen to be one of those whom the writer has specially honoured with her attention and selected as a target for her midnight raid. Difficult though it is for me completely to defend myself from such a widespread range of mischief, I must try through your organ to reach the ears of at least some of my friends who are on the other side of the Atlantic and have, I hope, the chivalry to suspend their judgment about the veracity of these shocking statements, made by a casual tourist against a whole people, before lightly believing them to be honourable.

For my own defence, I shall use the following extract from a paper written by Mr. Natarajan, one of the most fearless critics of our social evils. He has incidentally dealt with the incriminating allegation against me deliberately concocted by Miss Mayo out of a few sentences from my contribution of Keyserling's *Book of Marriage*—cleverly burgling away their true meaning and shaping them into an utterly false testimony for her own nefarious purpose. Mr. Natarajan writes as follows:—

"Tagore sets forth his own ideal of marriage in five long pages at the end of his paper (Keyserling, pp. 117, etc.). 'Let me,' he says, 'as an individual Indian, offer in conclusion my own personal contribution to the discussion of the marriage question generally.' He holds that the marriage system all over the world—and not only in India—from the earliest ages till now, is a barrier in the way of the true union of man and woman, which is possible only when 'society shall be able to offer a large field for the creative work of women's special faculty without detracting the creative work in the home.'

"If Miss Katherine Mayo was not a purblind propagandist but an honest inquirer, and if she had not the patience to read Tagore's essay, she might have asked anyone in Calcutta what the age of marriage of girls is in Tagore's own family. That she was determined to discredit the poet is evident."

Let me ask some of your readers to read my paper on Hindu marriage in Keyserling's book and challenge, in fairness to me, Miss Mayo to prove that it was my own opinion, as she asserts, that child marriage is "a flower of the sublimated spirit, a conquest over sexuality and materialism won by exalted intellect for the eugenic uplift of the race," implying "the conviction, simply, that Indian women must be securely bound and delivered before their womanhood is upon them, if they are to be kept in hand."

Let me in conclusion draw the attention of your readers to another amazing piece of false statement in which she introduces me, with a sneer, as a defender of the "Aruvedic" system of medicine against Western medical science. Let her prove this libel if she can.

There are other numerous witnesses who, like myself, if they find their access to the Western readers, will be able to place their complaints before them, informing them how their views have been misinterpreted, their words mutilated, and facts tortured into a deformity which is worse than untruth.

RABINDRANATH TAGORE.

Appendix II

A LETTER TO *THE TIMES*

An important letter was sent to *The Times* newspaper in London immediately after the publication of Miss Mayo's *Mother India*. It was signed by practically all the most influential Indians, official and non-official, who were present in London at that time. These included Sir A. C. Chatterjee, High Commissioner for India; Sir Tej Bahadur Sapru, ex-Member of the Viceroy's Executive Council; Sir Chimanlal Setalvad, ex-Member of the Executive Council of the Governor of Bombay; Mr. Sachchidananda Sinha, ex-Member of the Executive Council of the Governor of Bihar and Orissa; Sir M. M. Bhowanagree; Mr. Dube, Barrister-at-Law, practising before His Majesty's Privy Council; Mr. Kamat, Member of the Royal Commission for Agriculture; and all the Indian Members of the Council of the Secretary of State for India, namely, Sir Mahomed Rafique, Mr. S. N. Mullick, and Dr. Paranjpye. The letter ran as follows:—

Our attention has been drawn to the recent publication entitled *Mother India*, by an American tourist, Miss Katherine Mayo, who paid a visit to India during the cold weather of 1925–26. It has never been our lot to read a book which indulges in such a wholesale, indiscriminate vilification of Indian civilization and Indian character.

We concede that like other cold-weather tourists, Miss

Mayo was entitled to form and express her own opinions. But when a foreigner, who spends not more than a few months in our country, uses the material gleaned from hospital cases, culled from criminal trial reports and deduced from her own observation of isolated happenings, and seeks to fortify herself with quotations divorced from their context, and then proceeds on such a slender basis to formulate a general indictment against the character and culture of a great country like India, possessed of an ancient civilization, it is time that we protested.

She depicts the entire nation of 320 million people as physical degenerates, moral perverts and unabashed liars. If an Indian could have the temerity to pass a similar judgment on any nation of the West, after but a few months' residence in any country in Europe or America, and to indict the Western people, their civilization and character on the strength of the reports of sensational cases and crimes, moral perversions and physical degeneracy as evidenced by the proceedings of the courts, hospital and personal experiences, official reports, newspaper paragraphs and other special instances, he would be rightly condemned as unworthy of serious attention. . . .

We should not have felt called upon to take any public notice of a book of this character, but when we find that the publication is receiving serious attention of the British Press to the obvious detriment of India, at this juncture, we think it our duty to warn the British public against what strikes us as being a singularly mischievous book.

The Times refused to publish this letter, in spite of the very great weight of the names of those Indians present in London at the time who had signed it. This refusal was bitterly resented by the people of India generally.

Appendix III

THE SLAVES OF THE GODS

I QUOTE, in this note, a passage taken from one of the twelve stories which Miss Mayo has given in her book called *The Slaves of the Gods*. At the beginning of each of these stories she writes: "This narrative is taken from real life."

Under this personal guarantee for the truth of her narrative, she tells a libellous story about two followers of Mahatma Gandhi, who tear the last piece of cloth off a poor widow, leaving her naked, and curse her in the name of Gandhi. She ends the story as follows:—

And it chanced as they pushed across the fields, seeking the highroad, that they came upon a solitary hut, and a woman in a white sari issuing from the door of the hut.

"Who art thou?" called the strangers.

"I am the widow," a frightened voice returned.

"Whither goest thou?"

"Even to the market, to buy food."

"And what is this thou wearest, thou thing of foul omen!" cried one of the strangers, laying hold upon her garment. "A Manchester-made sari, by the gods!"

"What is Manchester?" asked the widow. "It is my sari, the only one I have."

"You must give it up, none the less, and let us burn it. Off with it! Quick!" And he wrenched at the cloth.

But Sita clutched it tight about her, covering her face. "Who says I must take it off?" she panted.

"Mahatma Gandhi."

"Who is Mahatma Gandhi?"

"He who can curse. And if you do not instantly give us your sari, cursed you shall be——"

Sita stood dazed. According to the law of widows, she wore but one garment. To remove it were to strip herself naked before these men.

"You will not? Then on your head be it!" cried the stranger. "Cursed you are, in the name of Mahatma Gandhi whose disciples we be. Cursed you are, with the curse of leprosy. It begins on your forehead, moving slowly, slowly, down your spine, eating, eating all your flesh away in sores. See! See! The marks are there, on your finger-tips, now!"

With a shriek Sita turned and fled into the hut, tore off her sari and threw it from the door into the strangers' hands.

"Take back the curse! Take back the curse!" she screamed. But they, laughing, sped on their way.

Three days passed.

"Where is Sita the widow?" asked the market folk. "She comes not for food."

"Where is my mother?" asked Sarat's wife.

And Sarat, the kindly, answered: "For thy peace I will go to the hut and see."

But the door of the hut was shut. "O Mother-in-law, art thou within?" called Sarat.

No reply.

"O Mother-in-law, art thou ill?"

No reply.

"O Mother-in-law, thou art surely ill!" and Sarat opened the door

In the far corner, crouched on the floor, a skeleton figure, naked, quaking, staring with great burning eyes at its outstretched finger-tips. The fever-cracked lips formed words —but to what sense?

"O Great Ones! Not clean! Not clean!"

"What meaneth this?" cried the man.

"The two young men, disciples of one Gandhi—a saint—who sent them to take my sari—to burn my sari in fire—and because I would have kept it they cursed me in the name of their saint—cursed with a filthy curse that consumeth all the body in sores. It beginneth at the finger-tips—here—O Son-in-law, look! Canst see the marks? Are the Great Ones dead?" And the dry voice strangled in a gasp.

But Sarat, averting his eyes, tore off his scarf and threw it toward her. "Cover thyself, O Mother-in-law. I go to fetch thy daughter to comfort thee." He closed the door and ran.

When he returned, an hour later, with women and clothing and food, that door turned slowly on its hinges because against it, swinging with the empty food-jar from the peg, hung a small limp body—dead—choked with the noose of the scarf.

To anyone who knows Bengal this libellous story is utterly and entirely unthinkable! In no circumstance whatever would any Bengal youth expose the nakedness of a poor widow and curse her. The story has every sign of fabrication.

INDEX